The Psychic World
of
James Byrne

The Psychic World
of
James Byrne

James Byrne and John Sutton

Aquarian/Thorsons
An Imprint of HarperCollinsPublishers

The Aquarian Press
An Imprint of HarperCollins*Publishers*
77–85 Fulham Palace Road
Hammersmith, London W6 8JB

Published by The Aquarian Press 1993
3 5 7 9 10 8 6 4

A catalogue record for this book
is available from the British Library

ISBN 1 85538 309 8

Typeset by Harper Phototypesetters Limited,
Northampton, England
Printed in Great Britain by
HarperCollinsManufacturing Glasgow

Contents

This book is dedicated to the glory of God,
my mother Elizabeth (Betty) Byrne and
the memory of Edith Johnson Guy

JAMES BYRNE

Acknowledgements

I would like to acknowledge the support of my dear wife Mary, the tea, cake and perseverance of my daughter Dulcie, and the assiduous application of Mrs Patterson, my typist.

JOHN SUTTON

1

The Early Years

The neighbours called him 'The Pope'. At six feet and eighteen stone, Michael Byrne was a powerful figure of a man. Snow white hair, barrel chest, and the kind of temper that would start a fight in a waxworks. He terrorised not only his local boozers, but also our unfortunate family. Mike Byrne, born in Wexford, Southern Ireland, was one unholy terror.

Married to him for 25 years, and the mother of his five children, my mum Betty tells the story of a marriage founded on oppression. Being too young to remember, mum told me about the early years of their married life.

'We lived at 3 Ellesmere Place, Longsight in Manchester, the home of my father. Mike worked as a long distance lorry driver and drank the proceeds. If it hadn't been for my father we would have been homeless. You would have expected my husband to be a bit grateful. Far from it, every night he rolled in from the pub, his tea would be a ruined mess having been in the oven for hours. This alone was enough to enrage him, not that he needed an excuse. We all lived in terror of the man, the kids had to be in bed before he came home, his food had to be on the table ready as soon as he walked through the door. Of course, that was impossible, you never knew when he was coming in, or what state he might be in. He thought nothing of punching me, but he always did it in such a way as to leave no marks. My father was outraged at the attitude of this crazy giant drunk of a man'.

'Longsight in Manchester was, in the early fifties, a nice working-class respectable area. The houses were mainly owner occupied and people took a pride in their homes. If the neighbours had known what was going on behind the door of 3 Ellesmere Place, they would have been horrified. But my family hid their shame and told no one of the fear in which we all lived.'

There were five children in the Byrne family, three girls and two boys. I was the youngest of the boys and lived in abject terror of my father, for it was myself and Michael, my brother, that 'The Pope' liked to beat. My mum explained how our family came to leave Manchester and move to Bolton.

'Mike worked in Bolton driving for a firm there, he had to travel each day and of course the journey was made longer by his extended stops at the pub. One night he arrived home in a filthy mood. There was some water on the linoleum, and when he saw this his face clouded over in anger. He started walking round it and grunting, I was really frightened, knowing what was coming next. I had been listening to a play on the radio with my father, but Mike just turned it off and tuned in to a jazz music station. My father didn't like this. Well, it was a mistake, but he started telling Mike off for doing this and said if he did not switch it back to the play he would turn the electric off.

'It was his house, he said, and he wasn't having that sort of behaviour. I had never dared tell him about the beatings. Well, he picked my father up and shook him like a rag doll, threw him on the floor and was about to give him a proper bashing. The old man couldn't defend himself against that kind of attack, he had a metal support on his leg having been injured in the war. I was so scared he could kill him, I grabbed a big metal candlestick and smashed it into my drunken husband's head. The blood spurted out like a burst water main, it drenched my father and me. Mike didn't seem to notice, he just kept grunting with rage. I hardly knew what to do and in blind terror brought this heavy brass candlestick down with all my strength onto his head. It caught him just behind the ear and as it did so the end broke off and flew across the room. It knocked Michael Byrne out cold.

'When we woke him up he was a real mess, his head was an open wound and he looked like he had bathed in blood. My father and I cleaned him up and put him to bed. How it didn't kill him, I'll never know. The next day he went to the hospital and they put fifteen stitches in the gash. They also made my husband report the incident to the police. I was making the tea when they came round. This young policeman knocked at the door and asked to speak to Mrs Byrne. "Speaking", I said. Well, he started laughing, and I thought, this is odd. I was only eight stone in those days and five feet five. He looked at me and asked if I had any knowledge of an injury to Michael Byrne. "We've just had a burly six foot, seventeen stone Irishman tell us that you beat him up." It really amused this policeman. So the case was set to go to court, my husband stayed away from the house, father would not allow him in. He came, though, crying and begging me to take him back. So I told him straight, the only way we could live as a family was if he got a house in Bolton away from this area. I was very surprised when he did it.

'Of course, the court case never happened, he would have looked a right fool in the witness box telling the judge how a woman like me had flattened a giant like him. He withdrew the charges and we moved to Bolton. It was only the location that changed, he was still the same, boozing and beating me and the children up.'

The home in Bolton was to be the scene of many childhood terrors for me and my family. The intoxicated rages of our brutal father extended to systematic cruelty as he deliberately physically abused and tortured the people he claimed, in his rare sober moments, to love. I recall one incident which to this day causes me nightmares.

I remember being ten minutes late getting home one night. My father was very strict about that, if he said be in at 9pm he wasn't joking. So I arrived late, he was drunk, you could smell the booze on him. There was no use in offering an explanation, he listened to no one. He took me into a room, locked the door and tied me to a chair. I was bent over this chair, then he tore all my clothes off me until I was stark naked. He got a big broom, the kind roadsweepers have with thick bristles, and he gave me the most fearful beating. He hit me with the brush handle and pushed the sharp bristles into my back. The blood ran down me, I could feel it trickle on to my legs from the holes he had punched into the flesh. It seeped from my rectum, and covered the chair. As he beat me, I could hear my mother screaming outside the door, but she could do nothing. The door was locked shut and remained shut until my brute of a father had finished his evil task.

The next day my mother took me to the doctor, I was in a right state. The brush had torn great holes in my bottom and back. As he had beaten me with the broom, parts of it had stuck in my flesh. The pale, soft skin on my back was punctuated with black bits of bristle. The doctor was horror struck. Of course, we didn't want anyone to know that our father had done this, it was a disgrace having it happen. For others to know would only make matters worse, so once again we hid our shame.

My Mum tells many stories of the wild and brutal man she once called her husband. His name was notorious in and around the drinking dens of Bolton.

'I'll never forget one afternoon, the woman next door had told him the butcher had kicked our dog and swore at her when she told him not to do that to a dumb animal. Well, this enraged him when he was sober, so on the way home from the pub his temper was beyond control. He walked into the butcher's shop, grabbed hold of the butcher and dragged him outside. Well, his two partners followed intending to stop this. That was a mistake, he kicked the three of them down the road and through the front door of our house. Kicked them into the living room and demanded that they kick him like they had kicked his dog. The three of them were terrified, down on their hands and knees they pleaded with me to stop him. Well I couldn't do a thing, I was protecting the glass display cabinet expecting him to start lashing out at any minute. He booted these three out of the living room and round to the woman next door where he made them apologise on their bended knees for swearing at her. I've never seen three men run so fast as when they left that house, he seemed pleased with the afternoon's work. Not that he cared anything for either the dog or our neighbour, he just liked to beat people up and humiliate them.

'One night the police came round to arrest him, it seems that whilst away in Liverpool he had seriously injured a man. He told me later that this chap had shouted at him as he parked his lorry in the car park. This man had then been silly enough to follow Mike Byrne and, on receiving no response to his "Hey, you!" had slapped him on the back of his head, knocking his cap off. The police told me the man was in hospital, Mike Byrne had picked him up and broken his back for him.

'He would smash the house up in a drunken rage, destroying the furniture and ornaments, throwing everything into a great pile, before staggering off to his boozed-up slumbers. The next morning he would grab the first of my sons he saw and thrash him for doing the damage he, in his blind drunk state, had done. The whole house lived in mortal fear of the man. When he was away, as he often was on long distance journeys, we celebrated, we knew that we could sleep in peace without the threat of a midnight beating hanging over our heads. I got quite used to being assaulted by him, I remember trying to fall quietly so as not to wake the children. A difficult task when you are being flung down a flight of stairs.

'One night he returned from the pub in his usual filthy mood, stormed upstairs, dragged our eldest son Michael out of bed (he was only five at the time), forced him downstairs and made him watch as he beat me up. The boy was in a state of shock when his drink-crazed father pulled him by the scruff of the neck up the stairs and threw him into his room. A typical Mike Byrne night of booze and brutality'.

Mum told me about a gypsy woman's prophecy: it happened when I was just a boy, far too young to remember.

'I was cleaning the home one day when I heard someone knocking at the door. The gypsy standing before me said that she had come with a message about one of my children. I didn't know what to make of it at the time, when she told me that I had two sons, one "M" and one "J". "It is 'J' that I have to tell you about, that boy is exceptionally gifted," she said, "and when he grows up this gift will be very strong." It did puzzle me for a while, I certainly never thought about one of my children being a medium or a psychic. It just never crossed my mind at all. Looking back it seems funny how that gypsy woman could have known that. Amazing, but it did come true.'

When I was very young I was always aware there was something different about me. My mother had told me the story of the gypsy's prophecy, but it was much more than that. I knew, instinctively, that my whole life had a purpose to it. From being a very young child I wanted, more than anything else, to perform in public. Of course, I had absolutely no idea what it was that I was supposed to be performing. I just knew that this was my destiny.

For a time I emulated my older brother Michael and went onto the Lancashire club stages. Michael was a very young club comic, only a teenager at the time, and I was a child entertainer singing the pop songs of the day. The organist and drummer at our local club used to play the tunes and I, in the mistaken belief that singing was my forte, warbled the hits. It was harmless fun and mum came along to watch her two boys having a go. We used to have a good time together.

I recall with horror the horrendous outcome of one such evening attended by my mother and the inevitably intoxicated Mike Byrne. Our Michael was performing at the local Liberal Club, doing a stand-up comic routine that was getting lots of laughs. He has always been gifted that way, able to get the crowds laughing. Mother had come along to watch and father had insisted that he be there. He drank heavily all night, glowering at our Mike who was gaining a great response.

On the way home he dragged us into one of his drinking dens, a rough boozer near the centre of Bolton. I was really very frightened by this, and my mum and brother didn't seem very happy; we knew the man was drunk and when mad Mike Byrne was drunk anything could happen. He started by poking fun at me for drinking shandy. 'What kind of drink is that for a man' he said, swilling down pints of beer. He had an amazing capacity for booze, fourteen or more pints were no problem – not to him at least, it was the people he assaulted who had the problem.

After about four pints, on top of the gallon or so he had swallowed in the Liberal Club, he began shouting abuse at other people sitting in the pub. Some unfortunate man asked him to be quiet, an opportunity not to be missed by my father. Within seconds he was across the room and had him by the hair and was swinging him round. The man's friends jumped in to tackle my father, but that just made him more angry. He flattened the lot of them, like in a John Wayne movie, rolling and brawling in the blood and the beer. Let me tell you, we were glad to escape that night with our lives, but to him it was normal.

Kathleen, my elder sister, tells me that as a child I had tried to defend my mother against the abuses of our crazy father, although most of these awful incidents have thankfully been wiped from my mind.

I might have tried to stick up for our mother, but it was no use really, it just made the drunk more angry. In the end I became ill and ended up on nerve pills, just totally frightened stiff of our wild man of a father. No wonder I cracked, the many beatings I suffered from this obviously deranged man disturbed me, I couldn't rest I was so scared.

He would often make me stand in a corner of the room, said I had been breathing heavily as he was watching the news. You never knew when he was going to hit you facing the wall, and when he did, it wasn't a smack but a proper beating from a giant, powerful man.

The images of my drunken father creating hell on earth for our family haunt me to this day. He would roll home in a right state, having been involved in some boozed-up brawl, order our mother to fetch his meal, which had to be ready the instant he walked through the door, and sit leering at us, waiting for a chance to give us a beating. Many, many times he would throw his food at the walls, something wouldn't be quite right and he'd start shouting 'these bloody spuds ain't cooked', and chuck his plate at the telly or whatever happened to be the nearest target.

As I remember the horrific days of my nightmare youth I inwardly scream, the fear is still there. My sister Kathleen thinks my psychic powers developed because of the wicked thrashings I received from my father. What an awful price to pay. It was extracted from me by a drunken brute.

I think God gave me the gift I now have so that I can offer comfort and help to people who are suffering like I and all my family suffered. There is, in this life, a reason for everything. I believe God wanted me to know the pain and fear I suffered so that I would be compassionate towards my fellow human beings. I experienced life-threatening terror for the first fourteen years of my life. My childhood was one of fear. Today, when I try to advise those who seek my help, I can relate to their fears, to their feelings of despair, I knew all of that at the hands of my drunken father.

My family finally arrived at the point where survival meant escaping the devil who threatened to kill us on a daily basis. It was a task which required both planning and a high degree of cunning. My mum explained to me how we did it.

'My friends offered to help me, the doctor was really good, Finn he was called. I still get a Christmas card from him. His partner, Doctor Walsh, was very angry with my husband the day I took James to him with all his back ripped by that brush Mike had hit him with. Doctor Walsh went to see Mike Byrne. He wasn't anywhere near as big as my husband, but he told him that if he ever touched the boy again he would personally kill him. But we had to get away, I searched and searched for a house to rent, all over Bolton, into every estate agents, week after week. I found one in the end, but it was in a mess. My friends helped me, we plastered it, decorated it, and it took three weeks to put it into a state fit to live in. Then we had to worry about how to move in without that drunk finding out.

He would have murdered us all if he had found out what we were doing. I used to scrub all the paint off my hands before I went home, we were so scared.

'The police helped us move. I went to see them, they knew all about Mike Byrne – they should have done, he was always being arrested by them for bouts of violence, yet some way or other he got off. Even the man whose back he broke refused to press charges. I think they knew that if they did, the next time Mike would kill them. So we waited until he was off on one of his long distance lorry trips.

'The police circled our home and we loaded up a friend's van with our few belongings. I say few, Mike had smashed most of them as he saw fit in his drunken rages. We left him a bed and a few chairs, enough so that he could live, then with my five children, under a police escort, we moved away from mad Mike Byrne forever'.

Mum told me how the Solicitors gained official separation status for her and the children. We were still scared stiff that our father might come round and attack us. In time, the separation moved on to divorce, and she told me of the Judge's comments.

'The Judge looked at us and said that in his opinion Mike Byrne had been an extremely jealous father. This seemed to ring true to me, because all through our lives together, anything that the children had done particularly well, he had turned around and twisted in his drink-crazed mind.

'I recalled that my eldest son, who was also called Michael, was working in the Pack Horse Hotel in Bolton, and the boss of my husband's firm was going to the Hotel for his lunch. Of course Michael would serve him. One evening Mike Byrne came home drunk as usual, grabbed hold of our son and gave him a severe beating. The simple explanation he gave was that his son, during that day, had been extremely rude to his boss. This came as quite a surprise to Michael because he recalled the man entering the Pack Horse and ordering both meals and drink from him, for himself and his friends, and at no time had he done anything other than his job. In fact, he had gone out of his way to be polite and respectful to the person he recognised as the employer of his father. Mad Mike Byrne had decided that he had been rude to his boss and proceeded to give him a most severe and sound beating, dragged him upstairs and threw him into his room, where he was required to stay for the rest of the evening.

'I was determined to get to the bottom of this, to find out if indeed my son had been rude to my husband's employer. So, I went round to see the man himself who explained that he had indeed been into the Pack Horse and had been served by my son who had treated him with the greatest of respect. This gentleman explained that he had mentioned the fact to my husband, and he had told him that this was a young man that he could be proud of. But in my husband's drunken and twisted mind he had turned this round to mean something that it obviously didn't mean. He, in his deluded state, decided to expend his fury upon the person of his son. Probably resentful of the fact that his employer had found time to praise Michael Byrne, when he found no time whatsoever to say a nice word to Mike, my husband. One can understand that because he was notorious throughout Bolton, no doubt he terrorised his workmates the same way he had terrorised his drinking mates, and the same way he had terrorised his family. The man was an unmitigated brute.'

The divorce of my parents was another trauma in the life of our family. Not that the fear ended there, mad Mike Byrne would often be sighted driving his lorry near our new home, the home supported by the hard work and diligence of my mum. To make ends meet, mother had taken a stall on Bolton Market selling second-hand clothes. She told me how she did it.

'When we left that crazy Mike to his own ends, we had nothing, I even phoned the cruelty man. When he came to see me, I told him I had no money to feed the kids, they were forced to sleep together, we had only got two beds between us. I told him that such conditions were surely cruel. That man has remained my friend to this day. He immediately arranged for us to receive benefit, got us some furniture, a new bed and really helped us in our hour of need.

'In time, I began to earn money, I took a stall on the local market and sold old clothes I bought at jumble sales. I used to go to every jumble in the area. By the time I had finished, I had three stalls, at Bolton, Blackburn and Oldham. I refused to give in and my kids were always looked after properly. Without Mike Byrne life, any life, was like paradise. It didn't matter that we were poor, we never even thought about that, we had each other, we had our lives, and we weren't being molested, beaten and abused every night. That was sufficient for us. The Byrne family were a much happier unit than they ever were under the terrorising presence of mad Michael Byrne.'

Believe it or not, within a short period of time from his divorce mad Michael Byrne remarried. He married a lady called Olive, they lived in Bolton and we frequently saw them together arm in arm walking round the town.

Some two years after the divorce, mad Mike was killed. Whilst working in London at the docks unloading a lorry, the load shifted and crushed him. Rushed into the local hospital, he was seriously injured; he should have recovered, but due to his extensive alcoholism he failed to respond to treatment, suffered renal failure and died. The day that he died, his new wife Olive contacted my mum. The words were simple, she just said 'Mike Byrne is dead'. Mother, who had no reason to know that her ex-husband was injured, understood the message to be about her son Michael and immediately fainted on the spot. There was great relief when we discovered that the death was in fact that of her crazy ex-husband.

In the following days his new wife, Olive, began to make funeral arrangements. She contacted mum and asked if she and her two children would like to come to the funeral for, unbelievably, Michael Byrne had told his new wife that he only had two children, denying the presence of the other three. Further indication of his strange and alcoholically disturbed frame of mind. When mum approached us about this, far from wishing to attend our father's funeral, we considered it a cause for great celebration. No more would we be accosted and beaten, no more would we be abused in the streets. The reign of terror had ended. The beast was dead.

Thinking about that brute's death causes me relief to this day. I believe that God saw what this man had done, decided that enough was enough, reached down and snuffed out a life that had caused nothing but torment, trouble and pain to the people he met. Such abuse was terminated by the hand of God. That man served nothing in this universe other than to perpetuate the brutality and evil that is unfortunately present in life. I believe that there are in this world good and bad people, my father Michael Byrne was a bad person. He was an individual whose whole life was ruled by alcoholism and thuggery. I can only say with great sorrow that his end was a matter for rejoicing in our family. We were simply glad that the man would never torment us again.

People always ask me how I came to understand that I may have a psychic gift. Within four weeks of my father's death, I encountered a woman who was to influence the whole of my life. I met at a bus stop a lady called Edith Johnson Guy, who was a practising medium.

I left home to go to work (I was working for British Rail at the time) when, standing at the bus stop, expecting nothing other than the bus to turn up, an old lady came to me and said 'your father was an Irishman. He was a big Irishman with a very big drink problem.' I wondered how she knew this, and said, 'Obviously you must know him.' She replied, 'Oh no, I don't know him, but he is standing beside you right now, and in his hand he has an empty pint glass. He wants to tell you that he is very, very sorry for what he did.' Well, I thought this was mightily strange indeed, so I questioned the old lady, 'How can this possibly be, you must know him'. Giving me a quiet, knowing look she continued, 'No, I don't know him, but he tells me that he has got five children, and that you are his son, and that he wants you to know that he's very sorry for what he did.' I obviously did not understand how she could possibly know all this and thought that she must have learnt about my family in some way or other, or read about it in the papers, but she assured me that she didn't.

She also said 'I'll tell you something James, I know that you have got the same gift that I have, and that one day that gift will be extremely powerful, and that you will go a long way in this world, because you, James Byrne, are destined to go right to the very top.' This absolutely startled me, I had never met this woman before, I didn't really understand what she was trying to say to me, but she knew my name, she knew about my father, she knew that he was a drunk, she knew that he was an Irishman, she knew that I was one of five children, all this and she said she didn't personally know us. I obviously felt that she was in some way strange, she certainly was to me because I was only seventeen years old at the time. Having given me her address she said that I should go round and see her. I had no idea why I should do so, it seemed incredible, but she insisted, saying, 'I am a medium, and you one day will be one of the most powerful psychics in the United Kingdom because your gift is going to be very, very strong.' It was at this point in time that I began to realise that I could have psychic abilities, whatever those might be. I didn't really understand what psychic abilities were, but Edith Johnson Guy, as her name was, told me she intended to lead me and it was then that I decided to go and see her and accept the invitation. As a teenage boy I was very curious about all this.

The very next day, I went round to her house, she sat me down and we had a cup of tea. She told me all about spiritualism, mediums and psychic powers. I was a boy of seventeen years of age, and she was a woman probably in her late sixties at the time. Having explained that the spirits had told her that I was destined to be an extremely powerful psychic, she requested that I come along on a regular basis and undertake what she referred to as guidance, in controlling and developing my gift. For the next few years I was round at Edith Johnson Guy's house in Bolton at least three times a week, accepting and learning how to develop and understand the gift that God had given to me.

I will never forget that kind old lady, without whose help and guidance my amazing journey into the psychic world of paranormal experiences would never have begun. A journey that was to prove to me, beyond any doubt, that life after death is a simple and unavoidable fact.

2

A Voice From Beyond The Grave

Edith Johnson Guy lived in a small homely bungalow in the northern mill town of Bolton, Lancashire. I recall the first day that I went to see her. I was, as you can imagine, most intrigued by what she had told me when we had met at the bus stop. She said then that I had the same gift that she had, a psychic gift. This, besides causing me some consternation, had made me extremely curious as to exactly what she meant and how she could know. As far as I knew, when you died that was the end of existence, but her story about my late father questioned this. I had certainly no ideas about the other world that exists beyond our material one. I'd heard about heaven and hell, of course, but this was something else. This was someone who seemed perfectly normal, offering me an explanation for life after death, something I had never previously considered.

When I entered her home on that far-off day in Bolton, I little knew what was about to begin, for within a few short months I would be experiencing psychic phenomena, the like of which I had only observed in the strange stories of the supernatural on television. Mrs Guy spoke of many things to me, such as how mediums receive messages from the world beyond. We sat in her living room, and she quietly explained that mediums were contacted by spirit people who live in a land beyond the grave. I listened almost spellbound as her incredible explanation of life after death continued.

Probably, the strangest thing about all this was the plain

ordinariness of the woman, she just looked like a kindly old grandma. Yet, there she sat, speaking quite calmly of an existence beyond the grave, and she seemed so at ease. She told me that the very idea that mediums contacted spirits was totally and utterly false. It was, she said, 'spirit people who contact mediums to pass on messages of love, comfort and affection for those they have left behind in this material world'. Slowly she explained that the way to receive the messages, which she assured me I would in time receive, was to relax, permitting the spirits to access my mind and speak to me.

For me, that initial introduction was an extremely strange experience. You can imagine that as a young man, I was ill-prepared to be told that I was going to be contacting ghosts, for that is what she seemed to be telling me. I was also, I might add, most sceptical. I wondered if, perhaps, this seemingly kind old lady had in some way decided to play a trick upon me. In a very short period of time, I discovered that far from trying to trick me, or make fun of a young man, she was playing her part in helping me to develop my gift. She would do this by giving me the guidance and leadership that I required, to enable me to fulfil the calling that was to become my life.

It is totally impossible to teach anyone to be a medium. God decides who will be gifted in that way, and all the instruction on earth can never produce that gift. However, having the gift and developing it, to the point where it can function for the benefit of mankind, are separate matters. Mrs Guy gave me the guidance I required, and pointed me along the path that would lead me to my destiny, as a gifted medium.

She would often say, 'The way to develop your gift is to use it. Every day, you must search for the spirit people who want to speak'. I was advised to be aware of impressions. 'Look at people and feel with your mind. Thoughts will enter, images from their lives, aspects about them that are, or have been, of importance will present themselves to you.' I began to practise this and found, to my astonishment, that more often than not, I was right.

Sometimes, I would be talking to someone when a vision

would come into my mind of an area in which they had lived, or a place where they worked. I was so often correct that it soon became second nature to me to trust these impressions.

I used to startle complete strangers by practising this on them. I might say something like, 'Oh, by the way, didn't you once work at the bus depot', and be spot on. I was really delighted with this power, and became ever more determined to master it.

Slowly, as the days ran by, I got used to going round to Edith Johnson Guy's home where we would discuss many things. She would talk for long periods of time about the messages that she had given from the spirit people who came to see her, and about how they lived in the next world.

She told me that when we die, it is simply our material bodies that pass away, but the essence that is the real we continues to exist. I was slightly incredulous at this, but she told me it was like a suit of clothes that we just stepped out of and walked away from. That suit may be burnt, but we would still survive and, in time, wear another suit and be alive in another existence. For the spirit is eternal, the spirit that is the essential us, lives on after the material body has died, and continues to exist in a different vibration than the one that we occupy in our flesh and blood bodies. She told me that the illusion was not life after death, but the life that we now live, and that reality was in fact the world of spirit. She explained that the material possessions and goods we hold dear in this world are an insubstantial setting that simply enables us to live and to learn. For, in this life we are all merely passing spirits encountering and developing, prior to entering into other lives in the spirit world beyond.

During my period of guidance with Edith Johnson Guy, I frequently practised meditation. We would sit quietly, contemplating nothing, experiencing a total void in the mind. Gradually, she explained this void would be filled by the spirits who were attempting to contact their loved ones in our world.

We spent a great deal of time discussing how spiritualism, for that is what she was telling me about, assisted those who were bereaved in accepting the true facts. That their relatives or loved ones had moved on to a world in which they would be receiving the rewards they had so richly earned in the lives they had spent on this earth, was reality.

She explained that the world beyond was a beautiful one, where the colours of the rainbow were brighter, where the grass was greener and we suffered no pain, where there was no disability, where we took with us the understanding and the wonderment of everything that we had experienced and learned in our earthly bodies. Our mortal lives are to permit development of the spirit, we simply continue to exist when these bodies die and step forward through another door into the next life.

It may surprise many people to know that spiritualists actually do read the Bible. She told me, 'It says in the Bible, that in my father's house there are many mansions'. She explained this as meaning that there are many different levels of existence in the spirit world, and that when Jesus told his disciples that he was going forth to prepare a place for them, he meant there was a place for everybody in the world beyond. I briefly understood this, but was somewhat taken aback recalling all the stories I had been told as a child, about heaven and hell. It seemed difficult to understand, from the spiritualist point of view, that there is simply a next life for everyone. What awaits us in the world beyond is influenced by the kind of lives we lead on this earth. We forge our own destinies, make our own heavens, or create our own personal hells.

Mrs Guy explained that in the next world, we are essentially the same as we are in this world. If in this life, we have been an extremely violent and bad person, then in the next life we will be a similar person. We all have many lessons to learn, the opportunities are presented to us in our material bodies and we create for ourselves a future in the spirit world that is linked to our lives on this earth. As the Bible says, 'As ye sow, so shall ye reap'.

To enable me to accept what she was telling me, she would frequently offer illustrations from her life. I listened to her numerous accounts of giving messages to people at spiritualist meetings, and she invited me to the Bradford Street Spiritualist Church in Bolton to witness this myself.

I went with her one evening in autumn, half expecting to find a darkened room with candles glowing, and people sitting round in a spooky atmosphere holding hands, attempting to contact the world beyond with table rapping and ouija boards. The experience was absolutely nothing like this whatsoever.

Mrs Edith Johnson Guy took the service herself, she preached to the congregation about the peace and love that awaits us all in the world beyond, expressing her feelings of joy at the fact that eventually this new life would, for all of us, become a reality. For spiritualists believe that there is no such thing as death, simply a new life, a new beginning, in a world beyond our physical bodies.

I observed Mrs Edith Johnson Guy giving messages to the people who attended that service. Those who received the messages, received them with both happiness and amazement, as she advised them that loved ones who had passed before were there, and speaking to them of love and gladness, that the spirits themselves were at peace with their new life and concerned for those they had left behind.

Mrs Guy told me that one major argument against spiritualists is that they interfere with 'the rest of the dead'. This she assured me was a complete and utter misunderstanding. The spirits themselves contact mediums, mediums do not contact spirits. She said, 'It must be quite obvious that people in the spirit world will only speak as and when they want to. For it is their choice to appear or speak to a medium. No medium can issue instructions to spirit people, mediums act only as receivers, to enable those in the next life to communicate.'

It was explained to me that the gift of mediumship is effectively a rare one. Edith Johnson Guy told me that the spirits had expressed their wishes that I be guided along the path of spiritualism, for they saw for me a future as a very gifted psychic. This was all amazing stuff to a boy of seventeen, I was baffled as to how on earth I could ever be a medium, for I had to that date experienced no phenomena that would verify the gift that Edith Johnson Guy told me I possessed.

I was working at the time for British Rail, and each day would travel to work on the bus. Getting up early one morning, whilst seated in the living room of our terraced house in Bolton having a quiet cuppa before work, I experienced a very strange sensation. It was probably about 7.15 or 7.30, when the hand that I was holding the cup in became stone icy cold. I immediately put the cup down and shook my hand to try and regain the feeling in it, because it was like pins and needles running right through my hand. I remember thinking at the time, this is very strange indeed, I had never felt anything like that before. I finished my cup of tea and went to catch the bus to work, still wondering about that very odd incident.

That evening, I went round to see Edith Johnson Guy. As I entered, she said, 'Oh, it's nice of you to come James, I had a visit this afternoon from your father, he tells me that he saw you this morning, and not only that, he said he held your hand'.

You can imagine that I was extremely surprised, because I had certainly experienced a sensation that morning which had puzzled me all day. She said, 'He really wants to let you know that he loves you a great deal, and is extremely sorry for the way that he treated you in this life. He wants you to know that he is watching over you, and that you will be what you want to be, for he is going to help you.' She was making us a cup of tea at the time in the kitchen, and as she came into the room, said, 'Oh, by the way James, he told me the hand that he held was the one with the cup in it'.

This, for me, was absolute proof that there is life beyond the grave, for there was no way whatsoever that Edith Johnson Guy could have possibly known that I was sat in my living room that morning, holding a cup of tea, when my hand went stone cold. Indeed, that information could only have come from someone who had witnessed the scene, and I had related the story to no one. I then really believed it to be my father, for who else would have come to see me from the spirit world, who else could have passed the message on? It was an astounding piece of information that startled me.

Mrs Guy simply handed me my tea, and continued as usual advising me on the development of the psychic gift God had given me. For to her, this phenomenon was an everyday experience and in time, it would be so for me.

I continued to attend Bolton's Spiritualist Church with Edith Johnson Guy. As time passed, she suggested that I attempt to give a message. I was very reluctant, and quite scared at the idea of standing in front of a congregation and attempting to do what I had seen her do so many times, pass messages from the spirit world. I had absolutely no idea what would happen if I tried, so I simply sat in the audience and watched as Edith Johnson Guy took the services. She continued to press me to try, but I was very frightened at the prospect of having to give a message and put it off continually, explaining that until I had actually experienced the phenomenon of hearing spirit voices, I couldn't possibly hope to do what she did. I thought I would stand up, and nothing would happen.

Edith Johnson Guy explained that the spirit people knew I was inexperienced, and they would be kind with me. 'The spirits', she said, 'will come to you, for they know that you are a young man with a gift, who will in the fullness of time enable them to communicate with their loved ones who remain in this life on earth.' Nonetheless, I was reluctant to undertake such a bold venture, to stand before a crowd of people and pass on messages from the spirit world, I simply did not believe that I could do it. I admired Mrs Guy and would dearly have loved to be able to offer the help and advice she gave to the congregations, but I had no confidence in my prophesied gift.

One Saturday afternoon I was walking through the centre of Bolton. It was very busy with much traffic and crowds of people shopping and pushing past me. The furthest thing from my mind was being contacted by the spirit world. In fact, I think I was probably going into the shops to buy some cigarettes, being a smoker at the time. As I neared Deansgate in Bolton, I heard a voice that I had not heard for over 12 months. It was a boy called David who had been my childhood friend. David had been killed about one year previously in a motoring accident. I knew that he was dead and buried, yet I heard his voice as distinctly as if he had been standing next to me. He said, 'It's okay here, I hope you're all right'. I was incredibly shocked, it was unmistakably David. I looked around to see if anybody was having me on, but the crowds milled around and continued about their business, simply unaware of what I had experienced.

I was about to walk on along Deansgate astounded at this, when I heard the voice again. David said, 'Go and see my mother, she's got two new children'. I was absolutely startled, there was no doubt it was definitely David, but I knew for a fact that his mother wouldn't have two new children, he had only died the year before and she hadn't got any then, so I could hardly expect her to have any now. My mind was in a turmoil, I could hardly tell her that her dead son had sent me to see her. I considered the fact that I had seen her perhaps a month before without any new children, and it was extremely unlikely she had now. Perhaps this indicated that I was hallucinating, having auditory hallucinations in fact.

I was thunderstruck at all this, hearing the voice of a boy that I knew had died the year before. I tried to put it out of my mind, but the thought was there, 'Is this it?' I did not even tell Edith Johnson Guy, at least not at first. It took me some time to get to sleep that night, my mind confused as to the nature of that strange experience.

An odd thing then occurred. Two days later I was standing in a queue at the bank, when who should be in front of me, but David's mother. She came up to me and said, 'Hello James, how are you? I would like you to meet my two children, I have just fostered them'. Well, you could have knocked me down with a feather, I was absolutely gobsmacked. There was the proof that I had indeed received a message from beyond the grave, and that David, my childhood friend, had returned to tell me that he was okay in the spirit world, and he hoped that I was all right. To give me proof, he had told me about his mother's two new children.

When I related this experience to Edith Johnson Guy, she listened very carefully and said, 'Well James, your gift is now beginning to develop, you must treat it with great respect and always accept what the spirit people tell you, for believe me, James Byrne, the spirits do not tell lies'.

I could understand this now, and began to see that what this lady had been telling me over the period of the last few months was, in fact, the simple truth. That life beyond the grave is a reality, that the people who live in the next world want only to tell us that they are happy and at peace, watching over those they have loved in this life. The silly suggestion that they are at rest is just that. My mentor, Mrs Guy, explained that spirit people are probably more active than we, in our corporeal bodies, are.

Following this amazing experience, I decided to accept Edith Johnson Guy's challenge to take a service at the Spiritualist Church, as it seemed possible that the spirits would help me. Initially, I merely tried ten minutes towards the end of the evening's meeting. I will never forget the first messages I gave, and on reflection, consider these to be rather inept. What they did do was to prove to me that I had got a gift, for as soon as I stood up before the assembled service at Bradford Street Spiritualist Church and began to speak, the spirit people were with me. I could hear their voices whispering to me as if from the next room. Names, I heard them whisper names, but not clearly. My life as a medium began there that night. With Mrs Guy's continuing guidance, I undertook longer periods, passing messages to the congregation of Bolton's Spiritualist Church until, as time passed, I eventually gave the entire service, just as I had seen my mentor do.

In the fullness of time, the information that I was giving at the Bradford Street Church was becoming more and more accurate. I began to hear the voices very clearly indeed, and the content given was extremely factual, much more than just names, proof to the recipients that the messages could only have come from beyond the grave. I gradually became accepted at the spiritualist church as a gifted, if very young, medium.

One exceptionally clear message I gave at the church concerned a lady who had been married three times. As I stood before the congregation, I could hear a man's voice saying to me, 'That woman was my wife, she's been married three times'. The lady accepted this information and agreed that she had indeed been married three times.

The next part of his message seemed, at least to me, to be most unlikely. 'I was her first, second and third husband', the spirit said. The voice continued telling me that he had behaved very badly in this life and his wife had divorced him. Even after she had married him for the second time, he said his behaviour was wrong. Then, after the third marriage, he died and he was now telling me how sorry he was. 'Tell her my name is Norman, I died of a heart attack.' The lady was most surprised at the accuracy of this message, the content of which was totally beyond my personal knowledge. Indeed, I had never seen the woman in question before.

The spirit of Norman gave me one last message, 'Say how sorry I am that I died when I did, we were both happier than ever, just before I passed away'. As I told her this, the lady became overcome with emotion. 'That is so true', she said. Clearly, this was proof to her that her late husband was with me and concerned for his wife. A simple message, but one which brought hope and consolation to the recently bereaved lady who received it.

I shall always remember the first time I was invited to speak at a church, other than the one in Bolton where I had received my guidance. I was asked if I would take the service at Whitefield Spiritualist Church, near Manchester. It took three buses to get there, the rain was lashing down, and when I arrived at Whitefield Station, I was nearly blown off my feet by the gale that was storming about me. Arriving at the Spiritualist Church, wet through, I found the congregation consisted of only twelve people.

I stood up and began to give the service, and as I did so, the voices were extremely strong. Never before had I experienced such clarity from the spirit people who were attempting to communicate with the congregation, albeit that there were only twelve of them.

The first message I received in this service will remain in my mind forever. It was from a young boy who told me he had been killed in an accident. He said his name was Andrew, and that he had been celebrating his birthday on the day he was killed. On the way home, whilst riding his bicycle, he was knocked off by a car and subsequently died. The boy's mother was in the congregation, and I recall feeling so pleased that I was able to give her that simple message of hope from her son in the next world. The tears of joy that she cried as I passed on confirmation that there is indeed a life waiting for us all, when we will be reunited with those that we have loved in this life, made that awful journey through the wind and rain worthwhile.

Andrew told me that he died because his head had been damaged. 'Tell Mum, I'm with Annie.' I asked the lady who Annie was. 'My mother who died some years ago', she replied. I told her that Andrew was with her now and had been looked after. 'Tell Mum to stop worrying, I am okay.' The lady confirmed that she had been very concerned about her boy, and thanked me for the message. 'I think I'll get a good night's sleep now knowing that he's all right', she said.

As I travelled back to Bolton, I hardly noticed the wicked weather conditions. My mind raced with the accuracy and power with which the spirits had spoken to me.

For days after that service, I was on a tremendous high, I felt elated and delighted that God had selected me for the work that was to become the essence of my adult life.

My confidence began to grow. Indeed, following the service that I had taken at Whitefield, I began to believe that the spirit people were watching over me, and were ready to come forward with help, to enable me to become an effective medium for their messages.

At a service I took in Bolton Spiritualist Church, a spirit person came through who told me that whilst alive he had been killed by a gunshot wound. He said that in the congregation were his wife and daughter, and that he had got two children, but the son was not present that evening. I gave this information to the congregation, and a lady accepted the message, saying that her daughter was indeed with her that evening. The spirit then told me that it was Peter who was not present. 'Yes', she said, 'that is correct, Peter is my son.'

The spirit person continued to speak to me, telling me that when he died, it was totally accidental. 'Tell them I didn't mean to shoot myself', he said, 'tell them that I love them very much and that I will continue to watch over them.' As I passed this message to the two people in the congregation, I could see that this, for them, was an exceptionally moving experience. They were there that evening, still in mourning for the husband and father that they had lost through a cruel twist of fate. The spirit person himself was concerned that they understood that he was in a place of joy and happiness, and that he would continue to observe them, awaiting the happy day when they would be reunited in the world beyond the grave.

Messages from the spirit world have got to contain specific facts, incontrovertible proof that they are indeed from the world beyond. Airy fairy stuff, such as waffle about beautiful roses and a world of sunshine and laughter, mean and prove absolutely nothing whatsoever. Only verifiable facts constitute evidence of life after death. It is proving this and reassuring the living that is the main task of all true mediums.

One such message which contained verifiable facts, as outlined above, I gave as a very young medium. At a congregation in Bolton, a spirit person came through who told me that her name was Angela. I asked those attending the service if there was anyone who could accept that name. A lady in the congregation put her hand up and said that she knew a spirit of that name.

As I looked at the congregation, I could hear extremely clearly the spirit telling me that she wished to speak to her sister. I passed this information on, and the lady said 'Angela was my sister'. The spirit of Angela explained that she had been in the spirit world for less than 12 months, and that she found that world to be one of great joy and delight. She wished me to pass this information on to her sister, who she knew had been greatly concerned by her death. 'Tell her that I am okay, and I will be waiting for her when it is her turn, and that there is nothing whatsoever to fear.' As I told this lady the information I had received from the spirit of Angela, she cried and said, 'What you are saying, has given me great hope. She has been dead for less than 12 months, in fact she died 9 months ago.'

The look of happiness on that lady's face, and the feeling I received in extending hope and compassion to a fellow human being in this world from those in the next, served as sufficient cause for me to continue with my development. I began to gain great pleasure from giving public demonstrations, such as those at the spiritualist churches in Lancashire.

As the months went by, my gift seemed stronger and I gained a clear perception of what exactly it was that God had planned for me to do. For, as Edith Johnson Guy had predicted, I was indeed destined to become a most gifted medium, with an ability to accept messages from the world beyond the grave. These messages brought not only proof of existence after the death of the physical body, but also hope and consolation to the bereaved.

As people heard about my abilities, I began to receive requests to undertake private sittings. Someone would approach me after a service and ask me to go round to their home, to try and contact a loved one who had passed on. I always told them, as I still do, that as a medium I can make no promises, only that I will try.

One of the first private readings I gave was for a family of three women: a mother and two daughters. As I entered the house, the spirit of a young man came to me and said his name was Ian. I could see something that looked like a body hanging from a rope, it was before me in the room. I asked the ladies if they knew an Ian. 'Yes,' they said, 'it is our brother.' The mother sat silently. I explained that I could see a body hanging and as I did, the spirit said, 'Tell them it was an accident, I was only playing a silly game'.

On receipt of this information, the mother began to cry. 'Tell them I'm all right and happy, this is a nice place', the spirit said. When I told them this, it seemed to comfort them. They told me that my message had helped, and were pleased to receive proof that their loved one was at peace in a place in which he was happy.

In a relatively short period of time, my gift had developed considerably. Demands upon me increased as more and more people heard about this young man from Bolton who could contact the dead. Churches from all over the county wanted me to take their services. It was a time of continuous learning, with new discoveries almost every day. A time when my powers were increasing and becoming ever more acute. I recall my mother's attitude to all this, for it must have been quite a shock to her. When she learned of my new-found fame, she reminded me of the gypsy's prophecy, 'your son will, in his later life, be extremely gifted'.

'But it won't change you, Jim, will it?' she said with a hint of concern in her voice. Of course I did not know exactly where this gift would take me, but it seemed that my path was predestined.

3

The Ghostly Choirboys

My work in the spiritualist churches, taking services and passing messages from the spirit world, made me feel that my life had a purpose. I felt elated after each successful meeting, and was always pleased to see the recipients of my messages accept them with the love they were intended to convey. Often the messages would contain an element of prediction. Of course, not knowing the people I passed them to, I only occasionally learned about the truth of these predictions.

One such message does stick in my mind. It concerned a lady who had lost her daughter. The Spiritualist Church was not well attended on this occasion, so I was not really expecting too much dramatic evidence to come through, yet as soon as I rose to take the service a young girl came to me from the spirit world. She told me her mother was in the congregation and asked me to tell her that she was with William. I gave this information and the lady responded by telling me that she had lost a daughter and her husband, who had also died, was called William. 'Tell mum I was killed in a red car and four other people were with me, the accident happened in the morning.' This information caused the lady to shed tears of joy, she was so delighted that the child she had loved was alive in the next world and with her father. The spirit told me that she was only ten years old when she had passed over. This the lady confirmed. 'Tell her to cheer up, she will meet another man and they will be happy together', the spirit of William, her late husband, had spoken to me and made this prediction. When I gave her this message the lady seemed quite certain it would never happen, I had simply repeated what the spirit had said, so I could not comment one way or another.

Some two years later, I received a phone call from the lady who had been given the message that night about her future relationships. She told me it had been exactly right. This was indeed evidence that the spirits do not tell me anything other than the truth. It was very nice to receive such confirmation as so often I never know if the predictions which the spirits pass through me are true.

I was enjoying life to the full in those days. My new girlfriend and I escaped whenever we could find the time and discovered the simple joys of youth.

I was far from well off, but that didn't prevent Catherine and I from experiencing life. On Saturday nights we would go for a bus ride into town and have a Wimpy and a cup of coffee. I have never been one for boozing, the terrors of my childhood had frightened me too much for that. Much better, I thought, to go and see a film at the local cinema. At the time, Catherine seemed to agree.

We often went for walks into the green hills and moors which surrounded the mill town of Bolton where we lived. Rivington Pike was our favourite spot, and many times on a clear summer's day, we would sit looking out over the wild windswept Lancashire landscape that meant so much to us both. I was happy then, with my girl. It was all I had ever really wanted: a job, a home, someone to love me. The things that all young people dream of were there, within my grasp. Catherine did not mind my religion, at least not at first. She accepted it as part of me, and as we held hands she would sometimes whisper, like kids do, 'I love you, Jimmy', and I believed her.

My mother was increasingly amazed at what was happening to me. Churches from all over the place were ringing her up and asking to book me to do a service.

I came home from work late one Thursday night and mum

greeted me with a list as long as your arm, of spiritualist churches that sought my services. 'You'll have no time to sleep in a bit, Jim', she said laughing, but obviously concerned for her son.

Mum looked after me then, still does in fact, taking the 'phone calls, writing the messages down, washing my socks, ironing my shirts, cooking the food and doing more than anyone could reasonably expect. Without her practical help, I would never have been able to achieve half of what I did do – I was becoming something of a celebrity in Bolton, as more and more people saw my demonstrations of psychic powers.

The services at Bradford Street Spiritualist Church were now a regular feature of my life. For days after each demonstration I would be on another plane, amazed at the clarity with which I was now receiving those messages from beyond. The detail and accuracy of the information I gave was real proof to the congregation that their faith in life after death was based on fact.

One clear illustration of the accuracy and worth of my gift occurred whilst I was giving a message to a lady from her recently deceased son. Standing before the congregation, I heard a voice say 'My name is Kevin, I drowned'. A lady accepted this and told me that Kevin was her son. I then became aware of empty bottles, tablets, pills, that sort of thing, and I asked Kevin's mother why Kevin should show me these. 'Well, he was a drug addict, when he died he had been taking tablets.' The spirit of Kevin told me he was one of seven children, and this the lady also confirmed. 'I want to tell them, I am sorry for all the hurt, all the pain and all the tears I caused', Kevin said. The spirit continued with a serious message for his mother, 'Tell her it is not her time yet, not time for her to enter this world'. As I said this, the woman's grief broke through, she admitted that her thoughts had been on suicide. The total misery she felt as a result of losing her son in such a way had made her feel like an abject failure. 'She must go on living, tell mum, I will help her and I do love her. It wasn't her fault, I just did not know what I was doing.' Kevin's spirit wanted to comfort his distressed mother, yet without a channel to put through that message, his plea from the beyond the grave would never have been heard.

Those who condemn spiritualism and mediums should witness such scenes as the one described above, for without my help the spirit of that young man would have been unable to reassure his living mother and help her to accept and live the life God gave her. That lady having received her message from the child she loved, assured me that from that day onwards she would restart her life in the world of the living. Who can deny that this gift given to me by a power beyond our mortal comprehension brings peace and love to troubled souls on both sides of the great divide. Yet there are those who would brand psychics as devil worshippers, who choose to make it their life's work to persecute mediums. If that is all that they can do with the life that God gave them, then I and all other spiritualists should pray for their impoverished souls. At that early point in my development, I little understood the hate which my mediumship could generate. For often, in this life, it is those who profess themselves to be devout Christians who persecute and hound those who have received gifts from the God those self-righteous hypocrites purport to worship.

As time passed, I became more and more involved with the spiritualist movement. My mentor, Edith Johnson Guy, continued to guide me, ever more certain that I was destined to be extremely gifted. We would sit for hours and hours in her little home, where we talked about the world of spiritualism, psychic powers and life beyond the grave. She advised me on which books to read, and frequently I would be up until all hours of the night studying the subject.

This pattern of life continued for about three years. I would go to the church with Mrs Guy and her highly critical husband Alfred who, despite being married to a medium, treated the subject with great scepticism. He was quite a gifted organ player and often accompanied the spiritualist services playing the hymns. His almost total disdain for certain less gifted mediums caused him, on occasions, to ignore the proceedings until it was time for him to play. He became so adept at switching off during the services that we would often have to wake him from a deep slumber in order to get the music started.

I never tired of learning about life in the next world, the subject totally absorbed my waking hours. It was of immense interest to me, and something that I felt destined to do. I knew that God wanted me to do this work, I felt the presence of a power, far stronger than any mortal force driving me on. It led me ever closer to my predestined position, and I was a willing student.

Mrs Guy would often advise me on the development of my gift. 'Use it and it will become strong', she said, continually urging me to accept the spirit people into my life. Our relationship was not one of teacher and pupil, no one was ever taught to be a medium. Edith Guy offered only insights into the nature of my gift, leading me ever closer to the attainment of my psychic development and giving me an example to follow. Her never-ending kindness to this young man and the quiet spiritual peace which surrounded our long discussions, gave me a sound foundation, a rock to support the belief that became my life.

As the word spread throughout the local spiritualist movement that a new young psychic had arrived with incredible powers and clarity, the demands on my time increased, for I had developed not only my psychic gift, but also my ability to deliver messages from the world of spirit in an effective way. I have Edith Guy to thank for that, for she taught me the art of public speaking and corrected my errors.

Remember, at the time, I was little more than a lad from Bolton, generally used to conversing in colloquialisms, slang phrases and simple cliches. 'Speak clearly', she would say, 'Never say can't, there is no such word, always say cannot'. That lady changed not only my life, but also the lives of the countless thousands of people it was my destiny to meet and to help.

Churches from all over the local area contacted me to request my presence at their weekly services. Despite having to use public transport, I always considered it my calling and duty to attend. This was obviously not always easy. I was then working for British Railways delivering parcels, a full-time and demanding job. Quite often, I would be totally worn out with the physical strain of full-time employment, along with studying and demonstrating my gift in and around the spiritualist churches of Lancashire.

A further development followed the increasing acceptance of my psychic powers as being outstanding, within the spiritualist movement. Individuals would contact me to request private readings. I had never considered this as something I might be asked, or even expected to do. However, this method of using my gift was to become a major part of my early life's work.

One of the very first readings I ever gave was to a man called John in Blackburn, Lancashire. I had been conducting a service at the local spiritualist church in Blackburn and this man, who seemed very distressed, came and asked me if it was possible for me to give him a private reading. This I agreed to do the following week, as it was not really possible for me to give private readings after a public demonstration. That would be making demands on my gift, which were beyond acceptance.

I recall quite well the overwhelming feeling of despair that flowed over me as I entered John's house, a simple terraced home in the centre of Blackburn. I immediately sensed a spirit person come to me and say, 'My name is Elsie'. I passed this information to John, whose eyes filled with tears. 'That's my wife, she's not been dead long, and I do miss her.' I explained that she was with me, and wanted him to know that she was happy in the next life, and wished him to continue living. I wondered why she would say that. 'I've been intending to kill myself, I miss her so much', John said.

John told me that as he sat alone one night, planning his own end, he suddenly felt that he had to go to the local spiritualist church. He had never been to such a place before, but decided, on impulse, to go. It was the night that I was taking the service, and he told me that what I had said about the world beyond, and the messages that I had given to people in the congregation, had given him a great deal of hope. Our subsequent meeting had resulted in his request for a private reading. As I sat in his tiny front room, I could clearly hear the voice of his departed wife telling me to comfort her husband. 'Tell him, he's going to be all right, he'll come through all this grief and his life has got real meaning.'

For some years after that night, I would see John at Blackburn Spiritualist Church, and he would often tell me how my message of hope from his late wife had probably saved his life. The use of my gift to benefit others gave me immense satisfaction. I never see John now, but I know that he went on to live a life of fulfilment, as he was intended to do. There is a purpose to everything which happens in life, a reason which is beyond our understanding. God really does move in mysterious ways, his wonders to perform. Had it not been for John receiving that impulse, that suggestion from the world beyond to attend the Spiritualist Church in Blackburn where I was passing messages and conducting the service before the congregation, it may have been that he could have terminated his life when it was his destiny to continue living.

People I meet who want me to give them readings often ask if I can differentiate between good and evil spirits. The answer lies with Mrs Guy who taught me all those years ago, 'always be in control of the nature of the messages your spirit control is passing to you'. It might not sound plausible, but I have never been approached by a spirit with evil intent, my spirit control will not permit that to happen. I only ever give out messages that are constructively helpful to those who seek my guidance. I believe that God gave me this gift to comfort and help those in distress, such as John from Blackburn who had planned to end his life in utter despair. To suggest that evil spirits would render such a beneficial service to mankind is to speak absolute nonsense.

I was conducting a service at the Spiritualist Church in Hyde, Cheshire, when a spirit spoke to me about a man called Derek or Eric, and a lady in the congregation accepted that name. She said that Eric was her late father, who had recently passed on. From the spirit world, Eric explained to me that he had died of emphysema in his mid-fifties and he wished to be remembered to his family whom he dearly loved.

He continued by telling me that he was present in spirit form to guide his daughter, who was going through a very difficult time with her children. The man's daughter agreed that she was indeed having a great deal of trouble with her own daughter, and had been thinking about her father that very day.

'Tell her number 5', he said. The response was again positive. 'Well, he used to live at number 5', she said. He also spoke to me of Denton, which is an area near Manchester. 'That's where his house was, he lived at Denton', the lady told me. This was all positive proof that the message was from the spirit world. Eric told me to tell her the name of Alan, 'that's my brother', she confirmed. Eric simply wished to reassure his daughter that her troubles would eventually be resolved. The spirit of Eric explained that he was watching over those he loved from the next world, and would ensure that they came to no harm.

It absolutely and totally amazed the lady in Hyde, who later told me that she had only attended the church on an impulse, having been thinking about her father earlier in the day.

This, once again, indicated that we are all moving in a pattern, which is guided by forces beyond our earthly comprehension.

A lady came to see me about this time, in a deeply distressed state. Her son, who was only a young man, had just died in his sleep. I remember she was so distraught, her tears flowed freely as she tried between sobs to tell me about this. As she spoke to me, I could hear quite clearly another voice, a man's voice telling me his name. 'I am Paul, I died suddenly whilst asleep, they just came and took me. That's my mum', he said, 'tell her not to cry, it was time for me to go, I was only meant to live so long. I was only 27, but that was all I was ever supposed to be.' I told the lady this, and she confirmed that Paul had been 27 just two days before he died.

Paul spoke to me again. 'Tell mum, I am all right and with my sister.' As I passed this message, the lady once again burst into tears, she was simply overcome with emotion and overjoyed that her children were together in the next life. What amazed this woman was the fact that the daughter had died before Paul had been born and she had never spoken to him of the child who had lived only hours after her birth. This was indeed astounding proof to the lady that life beyond the grave was a fact, an absolute reality.

I recall she left my house with a smile on her face, happy in the certain knowledge that her two dead children were alive and happy in the world of spirit.

As I extended my public demonstrations beyond the Bolton area, I began to notice that sometimes people in congregations did not respond to the information I passed on from the spirit world. This concerned me a great deal, as I had always been advised that the spirit voices told only the truth. I therefore wondered why, if the spirits told me true, the people for whom the messages were intended failed to respond.

I gradually came to realise that in a public situation, such as a demonstration in a spiritualist church, some people would be too shy or nervous to answer. It may also be that the information given was from a spirit who had long been in the next world, and that whilst the information would be specific, the individual for whom it was intended may have momentarily forgotten facts which, in an earlier time, would have been instantly recognisable.

Often, someone would come to me afterwards and say something like, 'Oh, that message about Fred from number 10 was for me', and proceed to tell me all about their late father called Fred, who lived at number 10.

I can now understand that they might be a bit bashful, but to expect me to go into an instant private reading after a lengthy public demonstration is totally out of the question. Apart from the fact that by failing to respond to the spirit's attempt to contact them, they had caused him or her some consternation, they had also made me look like someone guessing at names, a sort of fraud.

This still happens, and it makes me feel so frustrated, as don't forget I can actually hear the voices telling me to get on with it. Often, the spirits will say, 'It's for her over there', and generally indicate an area of the audience to which I should refer the information that they are passing. I can often identify the individual for whom the information is intended. This, however, is not always the case. Frequently, I am only given information which is pertinent to a specific spirit person. This information must then be accepted by a member of the audience or congregation. Once they do this, then the pathway is open.

This pathway permits the transmission of messages from the spirit world to the medium, i.e. myself, and on to those for whom it is intended. If, however, those for whom the message is intended fail to acknowledge the information that I give, then I, as a medium can do nothing. My task as a medium is simply to present the information and to pass on the messages. A failure by those people to respond is beyond my control. It simply means that the spirit cannot pass the message, and I, as a medium, look as if I am floundering around, lost for words and trying it on to make it all fit. This is something that I have never done, nor ever will do.

When I stand before an audience or a congregation, the messages that I give are from the spirit world. They are given to me by the spirit voices which I hear. At no time have I ever, nor will I ever, attempt to fit a name to suit any given situation, just to make it look as if I am correct. If I am hearing the voices incorrectly, then that is a mistake on my part and a fault in my mediumistic powers which, as good as they are, can never be perfect.

It should, therefore, be clear to any individuals attending a spiritualist church, public demonstration, or undertaking a private reading with a medium, that often the spirit people give information which is not immediately grasped by the intended recipient. It is one aspect of my mediumistic powers which will, for as long as I am undertaking this work, cause me great frustration.

I have no doubts whatsoever that for as long as I am standing on public platforms throughout the world, people will continue to come to me after the demonstration and say that a particular message had been intended for them. I will always say the same thing: thank you very much for telling me, I simply pass on the messages that the spirits give to me. The voices never tell me anything but the truth, as strange as that truth may sometimes be.

I was taking a service one wet Thursday night in the middle of Manchester, when I heard a spirit voice telling me the name of Banks. I gave this information out and a lady in the congregation said 'My name's Banks'. I could hear the spirit voice plainly say, 'Tell her I have got my leg underneath my arm'. So, as daft as it sounded, I passed the message on. 'Oh, he had his left leg amputated shortly before he died', she said, amazed at the accuracy of the proof.

It made the problems I had getting to that church more than worthwhile. As tired as I was of catching bus after bus in the pouring September rain, I had once again offered the truth of life after death to someone who was desperate for help.

Working at British Rail eight hours a day, and undertaking an ever-increasing amount of private readings and public demonstrations, tired me out. For a short period of time I questioned my calling. Physically overstretched, and under immense pressure to produce my psychic powers, almost on demand, I felt incapable of continuing.

My girlfriend Catherine had wearied of me and my continuous travelling round the churches. I did try to make her understand that God wanted me to help others with my gift. 'What about us, why don't you help us first?' she asked. Seeing all her friends going off to dances, having a good time, drinking in the pubs, and just doing what young people do in Bolton, caused her to question our floundering relationship. I should have known that when she had whispered 'I love you, Jimmy', it was only a phrase in praise of a dream that for me could never be reality.

At this time, I remember sitting in our living room late one night. I had been studying some books on spiritualism, and during the previous week had undertaken numerous private readings and demonstrations of my mediumistic powers at spiritualist churches in and around the Bolton area. As I sat in that tiny room, in a terraced house in the back streets of Bolton, weary and worn out, I began to doubt my ability to continue, the strain was simply too much. I was a young man but I questioned my destiny. I felt I had no future. Better, I thought, to quit now, get on with being a delivery man. Why, I wondered, should I waste my time struggling to be a medium? I was almost at the point of throwing it all away, exhausted and depressed, as I sat in that little room, lonely and desolate, with my head sinking down onto my chest. Perhaps I even cried a little.

As I sat there, I began to hear the sound of singing, a heavenly sound of harmonious clarity. Suddenly, I felt a hand underneath my chin, lifting my head up, and a young voice said, 'Come on, let's see a smile on your face'. I looked up and saw before me three choirboys, who were smiling. The sense of peace and love that filled the room was exceptionally intense. They simply radiated goodness and light. As I gazed, they pointed to a table covered in heavy dark velvet. 'Look', they said, 'these are your gifts.' The table was covered in jewellery – diamonds, emeralds, rubies and many other precious stones. Slowly, the vision faded from sight, I was left alone again in that tiny front room. But with me now was a sense of purpose, for this had been a message for me from the world beyond. I had to use those heavenly gifts to help my fellow man.

I discussed this experience with Edith Johnson Guy and explained the feeling of love with which those ghostly choirboys had left me. 'Always remember James,' she said, 'God has given you those precious gifts for a reason. You must use them wisely, do that and you will go a long way in this life.'

That vision altered my perception of the challenge I had to face to achieve my potential. No longer did I consider it to be a struggle, I was simply following my predestined path.

From that moment on, I have never doubted for a single second that my life's work is of great importance and my destiny one which I must, and will, fulfil.

4

Healing Powers

Edith Johnson Guy would talk to me for hours about one of the precious gifts which God had given to me. Explaining that someone with developed powers could perform psychic healing, she told me of the wondrous cures which the spirit healers made possible. 'You are a natural medium', she would say, 'the spirit people can use your gifts to do more than simply communicate with this world'. She explained that in the next world there exist healers who are able to effect miraculous cures for those in this life suffering from health problems. 'Healing is one of the precious gifts God has given to you', she said. Incredible truths all spoken in her calm, peaceful, matter-of-fact way, the tone would never change – from speaking of the weather to discussing strange supernatural experiences, she remained totally and utterly at ease.

Looking back at those long meetings with that kindly old spiritualist, I believe quite sincerely that without her guidance I would not have accepted the call from beyond the grave to tread my prophesied path to psychic power. She helped me to come to terms with what would otherwise most certainly have been a very unsettling time.

Not that we as a family were in mourning following the death of mad Mike Byrne. That event had improved matters considerably. But I was still recovering from the extreme traumas of a childhood ruined by physical and mental abuse when I met Edith Johnson Guy.

Had it not been for her intelligent guidance, my path through this life could have been stony indeed. As a victim, I had sought the help of our most excellent and understanding GP. He had prescribed some form of nerve pills. What, I wonder, would he have given me for voices from beyond the grave!

I almost suspect that despite being the kindly gentleman he most certainly was, he might just have thought I was going round the bend. The question is still in my mind to this day, how many others with a similar gift to mine have failed to realise the truth. For without Mrs Guy, I would have been at a total loss as to exactly what was happening to me. I could quite easily have been lost forever.

I closely questioned Mrs Guy about her beliefs. 'Trust in the spirits, James, they will respond.' She had great faith in me, much more than I had in myself. Her help had enabled me to receive and pass messages from the next world, and she surely could not be inventing the suggestion that my gifts extended to healing. I was soon to be put to the test.

By this time, all our neighbours and half of Bolton knew about my powers as a medium. The Bradford Street Church was full whenever I gave the service, and my messages certainly seemed to impress the congregations. And so it was, when a young girl who lived next door to us fell ill, her mother approached me and asked if I could heal her. My mum answered the door. 'Can James help us with our girl? The doctor says there is nothing much he can do. She's been up all night crying, and they say your lad's got the gift.' Mum gave me one of her old-fashioned looks and off I went.

Lynne had displaced her hip bone in a minor fall. The doctors had fitted her with those awful-looking callipers, and told her it would be a long time before it was right again. The poor girl was in constant pain and was barely able to walk. Her mother invited me into their living room, where she lay in obvious discomfort on the large sofa. I remember thinking back to what my mentor had so often told me: 'Trust in the spirits, James, they will respond'.

As I looked down at the young girl, crippled and in pain,

I said a little prayer to myself asking the spirits to help this child. As I prayed, a strange feeling of healing, spiritual strength flooded into me. I stood there trusting, as Mrs Guy had told me to trust, in the spirit healers, looking down at the injured girl who grimaced in agony as she showed me exactly where the pain was strongest. Reaching out, I placed my hands on her damaged hip. No sooner did my fingers touch her dress than an almighty crack boomed out, echoing around the room. I nearly fell over with the shock, but no one else had heard a thing. The girl just stared up at me and slowly the tenseness caused by her pain eased. Suddenly smiling, she raised herself upwards into a sitting position. I could sense the relief running through that little body. Her mother just looked at me in utter astonishment, as her daughter cried, 'It's all gone, the pain's all gone'. Quickly unclipping the callipers, young Lynne ran next door to tell my mother what had happened. 'I don't know,' mum said, 'what will you do next Jim?' To that, there seemed to be no answer, at least not in this world.

I always remembered what I had been told: 'Use your gift and it will become strong'. So, as more and more people came to me for healing, I decided to set up a regular clinic. This was certainly nothing elaborate whatsoever, my mother just let me use the front room of our house. Each Saturday morning people, all sorts of people, would come round and I would ask the spirits to give them help. Some of these from those early days have become firm friends.

I was, of course, just a young man, and the blood ran strongly in my youthful veins, yet I had no time to spare for the pursuits of pleasure. Catherine had abandoned our relationship, aware that my life was dedicated to the gift God had given me. At times, I pondered the fairness of it all. People expected so much, needed so much, and it seemed my duty to respond. It still does, I never refuse to help in any way that I can. But in personal terms I have paid, and continue to pay, a heavy price.

Early one Saturday morning, when the sun was cracking the flag stones and I was half wishing to be off with a girlfriend into the green hills of nearby Rivington, a very sick man was carried to my clinic. This man could not stand without support and his two friends held him between them, lifting him through our front door. As he lay on the settee gasping for breath, clutching his chest and trying his best to look hopeful, I wondered deep inside how on earth I was going to help this poor suffering creature, he seemed close to death. His friends explained that for years he had suffered from shortness of breath, unable to manage more than a few yards without stopping for a rest. Of late, his leg had developed problems with circulation, so much so that he could no longer stand upright without help. As he looked up at me, wheezing and pale, I heard a spirit voice say, 'This man will be all right, tell him to stand up'.

The man was in his fifties, and I little more than a lad. He was obviously in deep distress, fighting for breath, and had entered under the physical assistance of two strong men. Perhaps you can imagine what went through my mind as I heard the spirit healer say, 'tell him to stand up'. If I had said that outright, I am sure his friends would have thought I was totally nuts. So considering the situation, I decided to respond in what seemed to me to be a more acceptable way. I had no doubts that the spirits would heal him, I just needed to present this healing in a way that would enable all involved to accept it.

I reached down and placed my hands upon his chest, and as I did so I could hear his breathing ease. Within fifteen minutes he was sitting upright. 'Now get up and walk', I said, half fearing that he might fall over. I should have known that my voices never tell me lies. He stood and walked from my house, much to the open-mouthed amazement of his two friends who stared in utter wonderment at the incredible sight they had just witnessed. I was even impressed myself. To think I had questioned Mrs Guy and been fool enough to harbour doubts. I was certainly convinced now, and so was the patient.

That man's name is George Ratcliffe, and to this day he has never again suffered the agonies which brought him to me all those years ago. In fact, we have become very good friends. He only lives a short distance from my mother's home and often pops round to see me. He is so well now, that sometimes he attends my public demonstrations and takes the radio mike around the audience.

Some people have accused me of just being in this for the money. I never have, nor ever will, charge for healing. God gave me this gift to help the sick, not to swell my bank balance. In fact, I know of no spiritualist healer who does charge the sick. It simply is not done. Though I often think mother could sell tea and coffee some Saturday mornings when the house is full – she could certainly make a fortune out of that!

Most people think I am a faith healer, but this is not so. It makes no difference to the spirits whether you believe in them or not. It's much like not believing in the rain – you're still going to get wet, whether you believe or not.

I remember one young man came to my Saturday clinic complaining of severe headaches. He swaggered in, a six-inch sneer nailed firmly on his disbelieving face. It was perfectly obvious that someone had persuaded him to come and see me. From his look, I could tell he thought I was a charlatan. It was not an auspicious greeting. His opening line was something like, 'I think this is a load of rubbish, but I have tried everything else'. You can't imagine someone saying that to a Harley Street specialist at the initial diagnostic session, but people think it's all right to say it to me, and I charge nothing.

This man lived locally and had heard about my healing powers but, probably out of fear of looking soft, he had to announce his disbelief before letting me get on with it. He told me that his life was barely worth living, he was in such constant pain from headaches. So, despite the initial bravado, he was a man in need of help. The doctors had tried everything, and nothing seemed to work. As I placed my hands on his head, I could hear a spirit voice say, 'He's going to be all right, tell him he'll soon be wearing a uniform'. I told this to the young man, who just looked at me as though I was stupid. He had been unable to work for months due to his suffering.

Some weeks later he came round to the house to tell me that, not only had his pain eased almost totally, he had now got a full-time job as a postman, wearing a uniform. I still see Barry Barnes around Bolton, and to this day he has never again suffered the constant pain of those awful headaches. Proof indeed that, believe it or not, spiritual healing works.

It does not, unfortunately, work for everyone. Why this is so, I just do not know. Sometimes I lay my hands on a sick person and nothing happens, no surge of power, no healing message, just nothing. In such cases, I can only offer my prayers that all will be well. Perhaps it is my inability to attune to that individual's personal vibrations.

Being a healer can often cause me great personal stress, as people expect so much, almost miracles. I can only tell them the truth that I am told by my spirit guides. Often, I have to conceal messages that would cause distress to those seeking my help. I would certainly never tell anyone that they or a loved one were about to die. The spirits do tell me, but that is a secret which I cannot tell. No true spiritualist medium would ever say anything so awful, yet sometimes that truth does come through. In this life, we can all be sure of only one thing, and that is the fact we are all going to die. Strange that this, then, is the one thing most people are absolutely terrified of. So scared are some people of dying that they deny the truth of life after death. Different people tell me on a regular basis that when we die, we cease to exist. I suppose this might enable them to get on with their lives, happy in the mistaken belief that no matter what they do, death will wipe the slate clean, and that in time, they and their deeds will be totally forgotten.

Yet a belief in life after death is the basis of all religions. Some particularly rigid religions, go so far as to preach that if you do not accept their particular brand of beliefs as being the final word, then you're off to burn in Hell. People who profess this type of religious fanaticism should, in my considered opinion, seriously examine the ethics of uttering such blatant nonsense. How on God's earth is it possible that poor souls living lives of deprivation and hardship in the frozen arctic wastelands can be condemned to hellfire and damnation, because someone on a born-again mission failed to call at their igloo with the truth.

Yet this is essentially what they do say, and millions of lost souls, seeking an answer, accept these teachings as the word of God. In my opinion, any link with the truth is little more than an illusion, acceptable only to the most gullible.

The simple truth is that the next life is a fact. We all go there as certainly as we all die, one door closes and another opens. But, being human, I can understand the fear, it is the fear of the unknown.

How much people fear death was brought home to me by a young married couple who came seeking help. Their child, a baby boy called Anthony, had become so seriously ill that he was in intensive care at nearby Pendlebury Hospital. They wanted me to save this child, wanted me to tell them that all will be well and that he would live. I remember, quite distinctly, the feeling of utter despair that seemed to ooze from them as they stood shuffling their feet, bedraggled and wet from the autumn rain, standing at our front door asking me, a total stranger, to help them.

It must have been that I was their last hope, the doctors had given Anthony no chance to live, and really it was more a matter of time than anything else. Of course, I went with them, how could I refuse, knowing deep inside that if the spirits told me the boy was to die, it was a message I could not pass. Few people can realise the personal pain that this causes. Perhaps doctors experience similar stress when they inform patients that their case is hopeless. Yet even they may be proved wrong. When I am told death is imminent, then that is final. The spirits simply never tell me lies. It is a burden I, as a medium, must bear alone.

Dressing quickly in a gown and cap, wearing a mask to prevent cross infection, I was taken into Pendlebury Hospital's Intensive Care Unit. The little boy lay still, barely breathing. A nurse at his side looked at me and slowly shook her head, as if to say there is nothing whatsoever that you can do. The young couple, tears streaming down their faces, held hands and muttered what sounded to me like the Lord's Prayer. As I stood gazing down at that little wasted body, I could hear a spirit voice singing as if from the near distance, then as I lay my hands softly on his chest, I heard, in a quiet whisper, 'Anthony will live'. A feeling of total calmness came over me, for I knew then that the spirit healers would save this young life.

Standing at his bedside I led the parents in prayer, assuring them that God would save their child, that he would be healed, and so it was. I occasionally see that couple about the town, and they tell me that Anthony is now a strong healthy young man. Such news makes living my life as a medium most worthwhile. As Edith Johnson Guy said, these were indeed precious gifts that God had given to me.

People have often asked me if a certain amount of time has to pass before someone who has died can communicate with the living. The answer to this is simple, it depends on the spirit. As a spiritualist, I am frequently asked to take funeral services. I often recall the time when I was contacted by the Co-op Undertakers in Rochdale who asked me to conduct a service on behalf of the relatives of the deceased. I did not know the people whose relative had died, they were spiritualists but from outside my area.

I arrived at the cemetery, somewhere near Rochdale. It was a typical wet Wednesday in late February, slate grey skies with a fine mist of Lancashire rain heavy in the air. The funeral cortege entered the grounds and as the mourners gathered around the open grave, I began to read the service.

One gentleman in particular seemed extremely distressed, he was crying and wringing his hands. The poor man, I thought, he must really have loved this lady that we were there to bury. No sooner had I thought that, than a spirit voice said to me, 'Look at that fraud, he's not sad, crocodile tears that's what they are, he never loved me when I was alive, look at him now trying to impress his friends'. Well, I couldn't read the words on the page, I repeated the same line three times, but the spirit would not be quiet. I kept asking her, mentally pleading with her to let me conduct this solemn service. 'I'm in that box, that's me in there, I'm Elizabeth', the spirit said.

In the end, I closed the book and, trying to ignore the spirit's continuous flow of insults, all aimed at this man and the other mourners. I spoke what I hoped were words of condolence. I had, though, great difficulty in keeping a straight face when the man in question tried to climb into the grave with the coffin, and I could hear nothing but the spirit of Elizabeth shrieking with laughter at his antics. Proof, at least to me, that spirits can return, as and when they wish.

To illustrate the point that spirits can communicate with mediums almost from the moment of physical death, I will outline the case history of a Bolton man I had been visiting for some months, prior to his admittance as a patient in the Beaumont Hospital.

This was a man of 71 years, who had some major medical problems. I had been giving him healing in the recent past and had eased his pain, but I knew that I could not cure him. As time passed, so the illness got progressively worse, to the point where he was taken to this infirmary and underwent quite drastic surgery. It was a last ditch attempt to save his life.

It seems that the operation had been something less than a total success and his wife, sensing that hope was slipping away, asked me to go into his private ward and save him. As I walked into the room, I immediately became aware of this man's laboured breathing, he was fighting for breath. A nurse standing beside the bed said, quite matter of factly, 'This is a sign that his life is almost at an end', meaning that this awful breathing problem indicated imminent death. 'He'll be gone in five minutes', she said. At this, his wife became hysterical, grabbing hold of my arm and pleading with me to save him. His daughter flung herself on the bed, crying and shouting for God to spare him. I knew the man was dying, there was nothing I, or anyone else, could do to alter that, but I thought I might be able to ease his passing. Reaching down, I placed my hand on his chest and as soon as I did this, his breathing returned to normal. The look on the nurse's face was one of absolute shock. No doubt, my spirit healers had come to this man and had assured him that his life was about to end. Spirits tell me that this comforts people at the time of passing which, given that we all fight to live, can often be a traumatic experience.

We stood there, at this dying man's bedside, his wife weeping loudly, and I unable to do more than offer a prayer to God asking him to take this spirit into his charge. As I prayed, the soft breathing of this man ceased altogether, and slowly his spirit body floated upwards to the far corner of the ceiling. I could see this quite clearly. As he looked down at me, an overwhelming sense of peace flooded throughout my person. The spirit smiled down and whispered, 'thank you', and in that instant he was gone. I couldn't save that man, but my spirit healers had eased his physical death, enabling him to go gently into the next life.

Another experience of seeing a spirit leaving a physically dead body occurred in the home of an old lady I had been giving healing to for some time. She had an incurable health problem, but using my powers I had eased her pain and prevented her from suffering.

A very strange thing happened in this lady's house. She had been worsening for some time, and at each visit she seemed a little closer to death. One afternoon, when I went round to see her, I was taken up to the bedroom and as I came near to her bed, she looked up at me and said, 'Who's that other man with you, I've never seen him before'. This did surprise me somewhat, as there was simply no one else in the room, just me and the old lady in her bed. I tried to explain this to her, saying she must be imagining it, but she would not accept that. 'He's standing behind you right now', she said, 'he's wearing a light green doctor's smock with a white face mask pulled down, he's told me his name's Carl and he says that I am going to be all right.' Well, I nearly fell over when she said that.

Years before, during one of the long discussions with Edith Johnson Guy, she had told me that one of my spirit guides was a German doctor called Carl. I had never seen him, nor had he ever spoken to me, so without such proof I had refused to accept this information as being true. Now, suddenly, after all this time I had finally been given the proof that I required to accept this, for that little old lady, only days away from physical death, had seen my spirit healer and he had comforted her.

Some days later I received a call from this lady's daughter, asking me to attend as she had worsened overnight. I went round as quickly as I could, but really there was little I could do, save pray for a peaceful passing. As I stood at the bedside, I could hear her final words, 'Our Jack's here. Oh look, Uncle Bill and Aunt Ethel have come to see me'. I later discovered from her relatives that these were long deceased members of her family, obviously there to take her into the next world, where she would be reunited with those that she had loved.

Slowly her breathing ceased, and with great peace and dignity her physical body died. Some two minutes or so after the cessation of her life in this material world, I saw perfectly plainly her spirit body standing beside me only three or four feet away, her face radiating love, and she seemed to emit an inner glow of happiness. I looked around, but no one else seemed aware of this, the children stood softly crying, saddened at the loss of their beloved mother. 'Tell them, I'm all right, tell them I am with my friends', the spirit said to me. I could not give them this message then, for how can you say to people who have just lost their mother, 'Oh, don't worry, she's just told me she's all right'? they would think I had gone totally and utterly insane.

As a spiritualist, I could never tell someone that it was their time to die. I am often asked by the seriously ill people I visit whether their time has come, and it is something that, although I know the answer, I just cannot say to anyone. If the spirits say to me, 'this man or that woman is going to die', I keep it to myself. When asked outright, I simply say, 'sorry, I do not know that'. It would be cruel to wipe away all trace of hope and ruin what may be the final few weeks of life.

People do place a lot of trust in me, and believe that I can help them when all else has failed. I would never betray that trust, and even if I know that the problem is hopeless, I will always try to offer release from pain. I believe that we all have an allotted period of time on this earth and when that time is up, we must move on to the next life. I cannot change that, and my spirit healers certainly would not intervene to alter destiny. If you are meant to die, then quite simply, you will die. It must, and it will, come to us all.

Being a spiritualist, I do not believe in death, there is no death, only another life. Knowing this enables me to face the problems of this world, in the sure knowledge that everything happens for a purpose. What is meant to be will be. But even this strong belief is sometimes tested by the personal tragedies of this material world.

I had continued with my guidance from Edith Johnson Guy who, despite being almost 80 years old, had maintained her services to our local spiritualist church. I would still go round, perhaps three or four times a month, to tell her about the development of my gift, messages I had passed or healing I had given. Always, she was a source of inspiration, a keen listener with a firm grasp on her unshakeable faith in the world of spirit. She always encouraged me and I deeply respected her spiritual leadership which had enabled me to be of service to my fellow human beings, but I could tell that her physical life had become very difficult for her. She was increasingly crippled with severe arthritis and this caused her to suffer great pain when walking.

If I ever saw Mrs Guy about the town I could spot her a mile off. The limping, lurching walk, as she struggled on with a worn-out body, touched me with a great sadness. If I could have helped her more, I most certainly would have done so. As it was, all I could offer to do was carry her shopping bag, but being fiercely proud and independent, she was not even keen on me doing that.

Then, one afternoon when I called round to her home, her husband came to the door and told me that Mrs Guy had been taken ill. He had heard a thud in the next room and when he went in, found her lying on the floor where she had fallen. The doctors said she had suffered a severe stroke, and they had taken her to hospital. I was told that this stroke had caused catastrophic damage to her co-ordination. Her life as a functioning, self-motivated and capable human being was effectively over. It broke my heart to think that I would never again sit at her side and listen to her words of wisdom. Words that were worth more to me than gold, for it was that kind old spiritualist minister that had taken this green young boy and turned him into a medium. I tried to go and visit, but somehow I wanted to remember her the way she had always been, and kept putting off the moment when I would enter the hospital. Within a week, she had passed on to the next life.

At the funeral, I was absolutely distraught, the woman who had guided me, given me years of her time, absolutely changing my life, leading me to the spiritualist belief, had passed on. It was Edith Johnson Guy who was almost totally responsible for the development of those gifts that were to prove to be my life's work. Now she was dead. At that point, I doubted if I could continue, for I was effectively alone. No longer would I be able to seek guidance and help from the very person who had enabled me to become a developed psychic.

Then as I sat alone, contemplating my sad loss, crying unashamed tears, I recalled the words of that dear woman. Words she had used so many times, to guide and encourage me throughout the years: 'Trust in the spirits, James, they will respond'. I knew then that my faith would survive, it was as if she was standing beside me to offer comfort in my utter sadness, but I would never forget that kind old lady who had brought so much joy into my life, and into the lives of the many people she had helped over the years of her spiritualist ministry.

There is a commemorative plaque in Bradford Street Spiritualist Hall to the memory of Edith Johnson Guy. It says, 'she dedicated her life to the church'. She did so much more than that, and as long as I draw breath on this earth, I will remember her in my prayers. For without her gentle guidance, I would have been but a walking shadow of the gifted medium that I have now become.

5

Going On Stage

Coming to terms with life without Edith Johnson Guy to guide me was, at first, quite difficult. I missed terribly those long comforting talks that we would have, when I could question her for hour upon hour about aspects of this amazing gift which God had given to me. Now I had to face the future and cope with my continuing psychic development alone. There were many decisions I had to make, as life's numerous challenges presented themselves to me. My dear mother was the rock I had to lean upon, that homely, down-to-earth acceptance of her son's supernatural gifts never failed to reassure me that in times of need, I had a friend.

One such decision I had to make concerned my work. Full-time employment, church services, innumerable private readings and spirit healings, gave me no time to rest at all. I was becoming permanently tired out. Obviously, I could not keep up that kind of pace, something had to give. Then, as so often happens in this life, fate, or is it destiny, intervened.

I was called late one Friday afternoon into the Transport Manager's office at the BR Depot where I worked. 'Bad news, Jim. BR's making all drivers at this depot redundant.' I looked round at the shocked and disappointed faces of my colleagues. For them, this was indeed bad news. For me, however, it was a blessing in disguise, as it took all the pain out of deciding to quit and make my living as a full-time medium. I would be free to pursue my calling and earn my living as a professional psychic.

The flood of people requesting private sittings had, over the past months, increased incredibly. I knew I would have no problems generating sufficient funds from this source. My main trouble was that I had no personal transport and I sorted that out quite quickly, by buying a beat-up old banger for £60 through an advertisement in the local press. I had to be mobile, the readings were coming in from all over the area. It would have been practically impossible to get to some of the places by public transport, the time factor alone made it impractical.

So, as the owner of a late 60's Ford Cortina, two-tone blue and rust, with added string extras, I set off for Salford, Manchester, to undertake my first long-distance private reading. As I turned a corner into Bury New Road, the passenger door fell off. It clattered along the street, coming to rest against a lamp post, much to the astonishment of two old ladies, out for their morning constitutional. Making the most of this chance encounter, I took the opportunity to ask the old dears the way to my destination. The looks they gave me indicated that they thought I was quite crazy. The door I shoved in the back seat, and with the wind whistling through the opening, I continued my search round the back streets of downtown Manchester for Flat 6, Irwell Terraces, Salford.

When I finally located this residence, a sense of despair washed over me. The building, once a proud, four-storey Victorian mansion, had seen better days, much better days. The downstairs windows were covered in well-weathered wooden curtains, fixed firmly into place by six-inch nails which protruded from the rotted paintless frames. Some local artist had sprayed 'MUFC' in a purple haze of faded gloss over the heavy, once-white front door. An electric bell system had been tacked onto the wall, with flat numbers and names scrawled in ballpoint under the grey scratched perspex covering. With great trepidation I pressed No 6, half hoping that Mr Magumba and his friends would not be in.

Above me, I heard a window opening and a voice shouted down, 'You come right in man, we's up the stairs, top right'. My heart sank in my chest as I pushed open the warped, misaligned, dirt-encrusted door into Flat 6.

Entering the dimly lit room, I at once became aware of bars, prison bars. High walls seemed to surround Mr Magumba who, along with some of his friends, was seated on a lop-sided settee drinking from a can of strong lager. I suggested to this gentleman that sometime in the recent past he had visited a prison, perhaps nearby Strangeways Jail. 'Visited, man, that was one long visit, I only got out last week, been doing six years', he laughed cracking open another can of lager.

The things I had to do to earn a living in those early days as a self-employed psychic make me tremble in retrospection.

That first car was a death trap. I can clearly remember having to force myself to drive it. All my psychic hackles stood on end each time I approached the thing. Yet I had to get to the readings. The problem was solved one windy November afternoon in rainswept Swinton, when a large coal-bearing lorry ran straight into the back of it as I waited at the traffic lights. The passenger side door didn't just fall off this time, it jumped, along with the other three and the boot lid. In fact, the whole wreck practically disintegrated about me. A funny thing, though, the engine kept running – good engines those old Cortinas.

So, that was it, no car, no readings, I had to act quickly. Seeing an advert in the local paper which promised a company car to 'the right man', I thought I would give it a go. The interview was simple – are you over 6 feet tall and of proportionate build? I got the car. It was a job that caused me many sleepless nights. Collecting weekly payments for a money lender was simply not my idea of employment, I just could not do it. I would often put the pittance of money in myself when some dear old thing showed me her empty purse. I cried so much one night, it woke my mother who thought I was suffering night terrors again. I was, only this time they had nothing to do with 'The Pope'.

Despite the car, I could not, for any price, do that job. I think I only lasted about a month, and it was four weeks of pure torture. I saw sights in that short time that haunt me to this day. Heaven knows we were poor, but in relative terms we were rich compared to some of the desperate souls I observed in my time as a collector. The nightmares are with me to this day, I can still see worn out, weary old age pensioners showing me their benefit books and begging to be let off 'till next week'.

Life looked grim at that low point in my career as a psychic. Mum tried to cheer me up with her usual never-say-die attitude. 'Chin up, son, it'll be all right', she said, always ready to encourage me. But I must admit I felt like giving in. Then I met Rebecca.

I had caught the bus to Prestwich, near Manchester, where I was giving private readings to a group of middle-aged ladies. All rather well to do, manicured lawns and full sherry decanters. One of the messages had been about this lady's daughter. A spirit voice had told me that her girl was about to meet a new man, who would become very close to her. What it did not tell me was that this man was going to be me.

Rebecca was one of those strikingly beautiful women who startle you with their sensuality. Being a sensitive, I immediately became alerted by this fabulous creature. It was as if someone had shot an electric charge through my body, and I was getting such positive vibrations from her that I was almost overpowered by them.

'I'd like you to meet my eldest daughter, Rebecca', the lady of the house said, gesturing towards the red-headed beauty. 'This man's the medium I told you about, dear, he says you are going to meet a new man.' The young woman flashed her perfect white teeth at me, it was a smile that seared my psychic soul. The message was loud and clear, but it was not from the world of spirits.

I did not have to catch the bus back to Bolton that night, though it might have been a great deal quicker, and it certainly had nothing to do with the speed of Rebecca's driving.

For a long period of time, she and I were lovers. We rented a flat in Manchester and she drove me around to my psychic readings. I even managed to save money for the first time in my life. The readings poured in, as more people heard about the accuracy of my messages. Life was really worth living, I had a beautiful companion who told me she loved me, and once again I believed this to be the truth. Our happiness was, however, not to continue. Late one freezing December night, when the snow was wisping down the deserted streets, she failed to collect me. I stood outside that lonely spiritualist church in Warrington for over an hour, but Rebecca never arrived. Like Catherine before her, she had simply tired of this continuous cycle of churches and journeys, round and round Lancashire and Greater Manchester. I love that friendly church in Warrington, but it's a long way home when you're cold and alone.

I took a taxi back to the flat we had shared, but she was not there. Her clothes had gone along with all her personal belongings. There was no final message, no scrawled goodbye in lipstick across the mirror, like you see in the movies. I was simply on my own again, in a world that expected so much of me and seemed unwilling to give anything in return.

The next day, I packed my suitcases and caught the bus home to my mother. I could not face life alone in that flat, in that place we had shared and spent so many happy hours. I missed that girl, missed her so much it hurt. But I knew deep inside that I had to continue my work, that this was the most important thing in my life, above everything else. At least now I could buy a half decent car, get from A to B and thereby extend my earning potential. Maybe that was why the spirits brought us together.

I will never forget her. The delight of that first meeting and the feeling of fulfilment at having a home of my own with a girl who loved me will remain forever a happy memory. But all things happen for a purpose, Rebecca had closed the door on our relationship, and ahead of me, another very important door was about to open.

I had been invited to give a service at the Spiritualist Church in St Helens, near Liverpool. No problem now I had a decent, reliable car and could accept bookings anywhere in the country.

That night, my messages were particularly strong, the spirit voices clear and the information precise. The congregation was both astounded and delighted at the accuracy and proof of the messages. At the meeting with the church leaders afterwards, a lady came to me and introduced herself. She was, she said, an actress. 'I think you should be a stage medium', she told me, full of praise for the way I had presented the demonstration. I had never really considered that option before, though I knew about Doris Stokes and her theatre tours. 'Go and see this man', she said, writing down a name and telephone number. 'This man has the ability to put you on the stage where I believe you would do extremely well. You see, I think you are not only a gifted medium, but you are also, in my opinion, a very gifted communicator'.

The next morning, I telephoned the office of Brian Durkin, who was the theatrical agent the lady had suggested I speak to. Brian invited me to come down to Leigh in Lancashire and speak to him in his offices. At that initial meeting, Brian explained to me exactly what it was that a theatrical agent did. He had recently enjoyed some quite amazing success, taking pop groups, such as the Caravels and the Dooleys, right to the top of the charts. He certainly was not a man to mess about, he knew how to get things done. I explained how I presented my mediumistic powers to churches and congregations throughout the country, and having listened to what I said, Brian assured me that he was most interested and would immediately attempt to arrange a public demonstration so that he could assess the potential of the proposed venture.

The very next day he telephoned me to say that I was booked to appear at the Theatre Royal in St Helens. I was somewhat taken aback, especially when he told me it seated 700 people. I had never demonstrated to more than one hundred and the usual numbers were about 50 or 60. The mere thought of getting up on stage before so many people simply terrified me.

When the day finally dawned I felt awful, I kept being sick, I couldn't keep still, and I was a real nervous wreck. What, I wondered, would happen if I got out there and nothing came through. That idea made me more worried than I already was, and I became desperate trying to think of a way to get out of it.

Brian was really good about all this, he calmed me down, assured me everything would be fine and generally helped me to cope. In the dressing room, I said a simple prayer asking the spirits to be kind and to guide me. Then, almost before I knew it, I was out on stage before a near capacity audience and after the first five minutes, I loved it.

The audience were most appreciative and certainly seemed to be enjoying themselves. To people who have never attended one of my theatre demonstrations, this may sound peculiar. Who, one might ask, could enjoy a presentation which is all about death? Some think it morbid and weird, but this is not the case at all. People often have a good laugh at my demonstrations, they are about life, and life as we all know has many facets. Obviously, some messages from the next world are sad, but some are very funny indeed.

One amusing message from the first stage demonstration remains in my mind to this day. It concerned a little old man in the audience, whose wife of forty years had passed on the year before. She came through with a message for him from the world of spirit. The audience roared with laughter when I told him what she had said: 'Ask him why he buried me without my false teeth, when I got here I couldn't eat my dinner'. He joined in the fun and confirmed that he had indeed forgotten to give his wife's false set to the undertaker. 'I've still got them in the bedroom cupboard', he said. Proof, however funny it was, that his wife's spirit was present, watching over him with love from the next world.

Brian Durkin was delighted with the response. He couldn't believe how happy the messages made people feel. I knew, of course, that the secret was that audiences were astounded by the proof I gave, shocked and delighted to have certain information that, despite physical death, life went on; that in the next world we would be reunited with those we have loved. This is why people enjoyed themselves, I gave them hope, proved beyond reasonable doubt that what Jesus said about preparing a place for us all was true. 'In my father's house there are many mansions'. For each of us there is a place, a place where we will be with people like ourselves. Those we have loved look on with love and affection, awaiting the happy day of reunion in the world of spirit. That is not a sad or morbid message, but a message of comfort and joy.

With Brian Durkin as my manager the world of showbusiness opened up to me. I began to move in entirely different circles than those which I was used to, meeting many of the biggest stars and being accepted as one of them.

One very special demonstration I did was organised by Brian. He knew all the names appearing in and around Blackpool and invited them to a celebrity demonstration. If I had been nervous before the St Helens show, I was petrified of this one. The guest list was like a 'Who's Who' of showbusiness, with some of my personal favourites in the audience. I have always admired Les Dawson, his comic genius never fails to make me laugh and there he was, waiting to watch me. Vince Hill was there, that great comedy duo, Les Dennis and Dustin Gee were in the audience alongside Black Lace, the pop group, who had a hit in the charts called *Agado*. Whilst they waited in the audience, I was backstage shaking like a leaf.

I need not have worried, both the spirits and the audience were most kind. Imagine my surprise when the first message to come through was for my hero, Les Dawson. A spirit came to me and gave me the name John. 'I lived in Blakely village near Manchester', said the spirit. Les Dawson gave me one of his funny looks, as if to say 'Are you having me on, lad?' I could hear the voice quite clearly saying to me 'Tell him, I was the landlord of the Lion Pub'. Les accepted this, 'I used to go in there when I lived at Blakely', he said, 'John was the landlord and such a nice chap, we were really good pals in those days'. The spirit seemed intent on proving his identity and gave me further evidence. 'Tell him Bradley Road and his brown Rover car'. Les agreed that he knew all this, saying that he used to live on Bradley Road and at that time drove a brown Rover car. The spirit of John, the landlord, wanted only to be remembered to Les, who had been a good friend to him in his life on earth. I think the message startled Les Dawson, it certainly delighted me to give it to a man whom I had long admired.

At the end of this demonstration, I was taken to one side by Dustin Gee who asked me to help him. He had been suffering from a heart complaint that was causing him many problems. I agreed to meet him at his hotel and give him spirit healing.

For the next couple of months, I would go to Dustin's hotel and do what I could. The problem was serious and, ignoring his doctor's advice, Dustin refused to rest. We would talk for hours, what a nice kind man he was, do anything for anybody, a real genuine bloke with no airs and graces whatsoever. One afternoon, I suddenly received a message from the world beyond. It came as a vision, I could see Les Dennis's name outside a theatre, but Dustin's name had vanished. I told Dustin about this, I even had the date. I explained that after January of the next year, the double act was over. They would not be working together ever again. Dustin pooh poohed this, saying they were one of the most successful comedy duos in the business, with bookings running on for the next two years. We said no more about that.

I continued to give Dustin healing during the whole of his summer season, and he told me it helped him tremendously. I thought no more about my prediction, until some time later, whilst watching TV, I learned of his tragic death. Dustin Gee had passed on to the spirit world. A sad loss for us all, for he brought much happiness and laughter to this life. I am only sorry that I could not do more to help him, for I regarded him as my friend.

Brian put me on at the Grand Theatre in Blackpool, a beautiful Edwardian auditorium I had often attended as a paying customer. My career began to look really promising as I played to many capacity audiences in some of this country's most prestigious venues.

Going on the stage did cause me some concern. Many of my spiritualist friends considered it an abuse of the powers God had given me. I even questioned myself, wondering what Mrs Guy would have said to me about it all. I remembered those long evenings we had spent together and recalled her accounts of attending public demonstrations at the Albert Hall, London, in the early fifties. She had told me that all the most powerful mediums had presented their powers in public.

One can simply not please everyone all the time, and whilst I understood the sentiment behind the old brigade's objections to my theatrical career, I also knew that I was following an accepted and long-standing tradition. I therefore resolved to put all my doubts behind me and, maintaining my spiritual integrity, proceed with a career which seemed to offer me a chance of success.

The more I thought about it, the more I realised that my chances were in fact quite limited, and I certainly did not want to be a truck driver all my life.

God gave me this gift, the same way that he had given Mozart his gift, or John Lennon his. Why, I thought, should I starve in oblivion, just because some people considered it demeaning to present to the paying public my supernatural powers.

Up to this time, I had accepted no payment for such demonstrations. Can you imagine Cliff Richard performing free of charge, night after night, travelling from one end of the country to the other. No chance of that, and why, I thought, should I be any different. Vicars got wages, free houses, etc; bishops had chauffeurs and mansions to live in; why should I work for nothing? When God gave me this gift, he also gave me a belly to fill. Any fool can starve in high-principled penury. So, putting all negative thoughts to one side, I determined to continue, besides I quite enjoyed the stage, and my audiences really appreciated the consolation and comfort those messages from beyond brought to them.

The Tameside Theatre in Ashton-Under-Lyne was staging a Christmas Pantomime promoted by Brian, with Bernie Winters playing the lead. As one of the *Durkin All Stars*, I was invited to the press call. This involves photographic shoots and harmless interviews, none of the searching stuff designed to destroy one's confidence which I would, in time, experience. This was actually a lot of fun, and most pleasing to meet Bernie and be accepted on equal terms. Something I noticed early in my theatrical career was that the really talented stars had no edge, they simply did not require it.

I was booked to appear at that theatre when the panto closed and my posters were up in the foyer. Bernie saw these and, taking me to one side, asked if I could help him with his back pain. He had, he said, been suffering for years with this and nothing the doctors did seemed to work. I agreed to try spirit healing which, like all other psychic powers, could obviously not be guaranteed to succeed. In the privacy of the manager's office I laid my hands on his back, asking the spirits to heal this man. He later told me that he had experienced a burning sensation as my fingers made contact with his shirt.

It was some weeks later that I next saw Bernie Winters, when Brian invited me to view rehearsals. As soon as he spotted me he ran over: 'Your gift has helped me more than anything', he told me. Of course, I was very pleased and assured him that during the run of the pantomime I would continue to give him spirit healing. On the final day, Bernie told me that he had Doris Stokes as a guest on his TV show, *Whose Baby?* 'I'm going to give you a mention', he said, 'you've certainly helped me a great deal.' True to his word, some months later in conversation with Doris Stokes on Network TV, he mentioned my name with praise. Nice guy, Bernie Winters.

The response to this recognition was quite startling. I received thousands of letters from all over the country asking for my help. People of Bolton would stop me in the street. 'Did you hear Bernie Winters talking about you to Doris Stokes on TV?' they would say, and I with a great deal of personal pride would admit that indeed, I had.

My association with Brian Durkin gave me rapid success. Often I would arrive at 700-seat-plus venues to learn from the manager that they had been sold out for weeks in advance. I believed that I was about to make the big time. Then fate intervened, to alter my life once again.

One evening, whilst visiting the North Pier Theatre with Brian Durkin to meet Vince Hill and his wife, Annie, I met a man who was to have quite an influence on my life. At times, it was to be a disturbing, if amusing influence.

I was introduced by Brian to the famous Michael Vine. It was, however, some time before I became fully aware of exactly what it was that this man was famous, or perhaps I should say infamous for.

Michael had handed me his business card. He too was a theatrical agent, one of national repute and, having been featured as a regular panelist on *New Faces*, he was a household name. At our meeting, he told me he thought I had the potential to go all the way to the top. I did not know at the time that he had the potential to go all the way right over the top.

Working with Brian Durkin had brought me into contact with theatrical success, but somehow this success had failed to produce the kind of rewards I needed. I phoned Mr Vine who invited me to his offices in Blackpool. There and then, I agreed to sign an exclusive management contract with him, he was such a very nice man. He assured me I was star material, and by the time I left his office, I was ready to order my Rolls Royce.

One of the first bookings I undertook for my new manager was at the Alexander Theatre, Bognor Regis. The weather was awful, typical English winter, thick fog followed by driving rain, sleet and snow. By the time I got to Bognor Regis I was weary. The journey had been a nightmare, and on top of it all I was stony flat broke.

The manager of the theatre greeted me with the news that we had sold only forty tickets. All that way in absolutely filthy weather and the audience was less than a good night at Bolton's Bradford Street Church. I could have cried, and I had to drive straight back afterwards, having no money for a hotel.

As I sat alone in that dingy dressing room, I said my usual prayer asking the spirits to be kind, and as I did so peace came over me, and a feeling of total calmness. Then, before my eyes, that dimly-lit cupboard of a room transformed into a brightly-lit, flower-strewn suite. On the door I could see my name, James Byrne, and above it a golden star. The vision was so powerful, I was really taken aback as it all faded away and returned to the grim reality of Bognor on a bad night. That vision remained in my mind, I knew that the spirits had shown me the future, showing me that one day there would be a golden star on my dressing-room door. In the meantime, my audience awaited, all forty of them.

6

The Theatre Circuit

The journey back from Bognor Regis was simply dreadful, I hadn't even got enough money to buy a cup of tea. It was touch and go whether I had sufficient petrol to get home to Bolton and the night was horrendous. The snow had thickened, making driving really hazardous, I was also physically weary having already driven the 250 miles down and demonstrated for two hours on stage. The car itself was no luxury model, certainly not the Rolls Royce I had envisioned at my meeting with Michael Vine.

For days after that awful experience I felt really depressed. How, I wondered, could I ever make a go of a career in theatres with such disappointing results. I knew it wasn't me, my messages were accurate, audiences enjoyed the presentations, yet success seemed so elusive. I spoke to my new manager who assured me that showbusiness was like that, there were bound to be good nights and bad nights. I sincerely hoped there wouldn't be too many absolutely awful nights like Bognor.

Michael booked me to appear at Bradford's St George's Hall, and this time he came along to compère the demonstration. However, that night there was another demonstration which he did not compère. That demonstration was outside the theatre and in protest at my presentation. As I walked towards the entrance, I could see perhaps 50 or 60 people milling about the doorway, handing out leaflets to the paying customers who seemed somewhat confused to be confronted by people professing to be Christians, warning them of hell and damnation if they attended my presentation. I stood and watched as this crowd of protesters stopped little old ladies who, no doubt, were attending the theatre hoping for a message from a departed loved one. Appalled at what I saw I spoke to the man who looked to be controlling these Christians. He warned me that what I was doing would lead people down the pathway to hellfire. My arguments were useless against this way of thinking: these people were committed, they were right, knew they were right and nothing I could say would ever alter that. It is just a shame that some people felt a little frightened by them, as I am sure they didn't mean to be offensive.

Of one thing I am quite certain: fully grown adults don't need this show of force from religious groups frowning down their established ecclesiastical noses at innocent individuals exercising their free will on God's good earth.

That night I produced some remarkable evidence of survival. A spirit came to me and gave me her name, she told me that in this life she had been a barmaid at a public house in the centre of Bradford. A lady in the audience accepted this information and told me that the girl was her niece. I always insist that recipients of messages never tell me anything. I believe it is of extreme importance that the proof of existence after death comes from the communicating spirit. It is of no use whatsoever for me, or any other medium, to ask questions of the people in the audience, that is just tomfoolery; charlatans specialise in that, and I for one will not accept it. If the spirit wants to pass a message then it is up to that spirit to give me enough information to enable the intended recipient to receive and confirm it, and it is my job as the medium to be receptive to the spirit's message. The message from this girl was extremely factual, and caused the members of that audience to gasp in utter astonishment.

I told this lady that her niece had been murdered, I described in great detail the way in which she had been killed and where her body had been found. As this information became more and more specific, street names, addresses, etc, two ladies at the back of the auditorium began shouting 'You've read all about this in the papers'.

This happens to me quite often. It seems that if I fail to get all the details right I am a failure, and when I do get the details right, I am a fraud. What can one do? I simply pass on the information which the spirit people give to me. I do, though, feel personally insulted when I am accused of fraudulently obtaining the information which I pass. If people really do believe that I read the papers and memorise all that detail ready to give it out at my demonstrations, fine, let them think that, but how, might I ask, am I supposed to know who is coming to those demonstrations? I would certainly need a phenomenal memory to memorise everything pertinent to any given area around a theatre, and the odds against me getting the messages right night after night after night, using such a fraudulent method, must be enormous. Yet some people believe this is exactly what I do, they just cannot accept that the only way for me to get such detailed information is for me to receive it from the spirit world.

I don't really care what these doubters think, but what I do strongly object to is being publicly abused by them. Some individuals seem, however, intent on impressing others with their arguments, no matter how ill-conceived these may be. I understand that people have a right to voice their opinions, but why insult me? It is a great pity that those who argue in public against me don't take the time to consider what they are accusing me of. The gist of most arguments seems to rest on me having a photographic memory of immense proportion. The fact is, I am very forgetful, and by no means a memory man. That gift was given to my comedian brother Mike – I am just a medium.

Returning from that somewhat unnerving ordeal, having run the gauntlet of many protesters and survived, I now had only to drive home. Michael and I decided to stop at the motorway service station for a coffee. It was there at Hartsford Services that I discovered exactly what made Mr Vine famous.

We were sitting quietly sipping our coffees, discussing the

events of the evening, when I noticed Michael becoming rather agitated. He always wore a long black mac, which he now slowly pulled up over his head, then, in a loud theatrical whisper, said, 'Whatever you do, act normal'. Well, there wasn't much normality about hiding under your coat, so I looked slowly round to find an explanation for this odd behaviour. As I did so, I saw walking towards our table two large, uniformed policemen. 'Don't look at them', whispered Michael, loud enough for all of the restaurant to hear. The biggest of the two policemen leaned across our table and peered into the folds of Michael's coat. Michael stared back at the police constable with a very silly grin on his face. I don't think PC 49 was amused. He gave us both a look of utter disgust, turned and stamped away. 'Bloody fools', I heard him mutter to his companion. It did make me laugh, no wonder he was known in showbusiness as the famous Michael Vine. This initial introduction to Michael's eccentricity was just the beginning – in time I would experience far more outrageous examples of this interesting and intelligent man's authentic approach to life.

On another occasion I was appearing at the City Hall, St Albans, and Michael Vine accompanied me. I hated travelling alone; perhaps you can imagine driving 200 miles or more, doing two hours on stage, then all the way back with no one to talk to. At least Michael came along, even if he did snore all the way there. I put a Motown tape on the cassette as we set off from Bolton. The song playing was 'Baby Love' by the Supremes. Michael instantly fell asleep. As we neared St Albans, I thought I would listen to it again. No sooner had I put it on and Diana Ross had sung the first line for the second time, than Michael woke up. 'Still listening to that tape', he said, yawning and stretching after three hours sleep, 'has it only got one tune on it?'

At St Albans I gave a message to a lady in the audience who had lost her son. The spirit came to me and gave the name Jamie, he said that whilst alive he had lived in the north east of England, around the Tyne and Wear area. Then one day on his way home, whilst walking through a park, he had been shot in the head. Jamie came to me in his spirit body and showed me his damaged head, explaining that this had been an accident. 'I failed to put the safety catch on the gun', he said. This his mother confirmed, absolutely astounded that I had been able to prove to her that Jamie was still living in the world of spirit. She openly cried tears of joy as I passed his message of love and hope to the mother who had cherished him in this life.

Towards the end of the second half of my presentation, I became aware that the audience was laughing at something that surely had nothing to do with me whatsoever. I looked round and saw, sticking through the curtains behind me, the head of my manager Michael Vine pulling an extremely funny face. I nearly fell off the stage laughing myself and completely lost the message I had been attempting to pass. I think Michael had been amusing himself that night in another part of the theatre. He was certainly entertaining on the journey home.

As we travelled down the motorway, he told me that as a young man he had served in the British Army, in the regiment of the Special Air Service. 'They taught us some incredible stunts', he said, and proceeded to enlighten me further. It was, he said, possible for him to leap from a moving vehicle, roll along the ground and get up running. A likely tale, I thought, but offered no comment, other than a statutory 'fancy that'. He at once took this to be indicative of my disbelief and promptly opened the passenger side door. 'I'll roll along the hard shoulder, you drive on a bit, pull over and I will meet you there', he said, attempting to climb out of the car, which at the time was doing 70 miles per hour in the fast lane. A brief struggle ensued, with me physically forcing him back into his seat and firmly locking his door. It took some doing, I can tell you that. The next thing I heard was a series of contented snores rippling from the depths of the ex-SAS man's somnolent slumbers.

Two hours later, as I woke him outside his home, he seemed quite refreshed. I asked him then if he had really been in the Special Air Service. 'SAS?' he said, looking at me as if I was totally insane, 'Who told you I had been in the SAS? You want to leave off the sherbet dips, old boy.' Then he slapped me on the back and waltzed off for a good night's sleep.

Working the theatre circuit with Michael was rather like being on tour with 'The Who'. You never knew what was coming next, I certainly didn't and I am psychic. We were walking through the centre of Redhill, Surrey, booked to appear at the Harlequin Theatre, when Michael pulled a ladies stocking out of his pocket, slipped it over his head and, without further ado, walked up to a police constable and said, in a deep theatrical rumble, 'Can you tell me the way to the Midland Bank?'

That very night, before a capacity crowd, he produced the kind of performance which has over the years ensured his everlasting fame, but I am not absolutely certain my public appreciated his antics. I was talking to a lady in the audience when I heard behind me the curtains at the back of the stage set open. Turning, I saw Michael Vine, recumbent on a grand piano with a bottle in his hand. Seemingly disturbed by the raucous laughter of the audience he rose, took a bow, and staggered off the stage.

At times like that it was difficult for me to prevent myself from breaking into hysterics. With Michael you never knew what silly stunt he would pull next, a really naturally funny man.

One discomforting experience I had with Mr Vine as my manager came as the result of an article in *The Stage* newspaper. This publication goes worldwide, and an international agent picked up on this. Michael received an offer from a promoter in New Zealand to put me on tour there. Ten consecutive nights, no rest and numerous TV and radio interviews thrown in for good measure. It wore me out.

When I first arrived in New Zealand, after a flight that seemed to last for days, the agent met me. From the plane we called in for a meal and a beer in his favourite restaurant. I was really tired, but felt a good deal better once I had eaten. The funny thing about this meeting which sticks in my mind was the coincidence concerning a certain parrot. As we walked into the bar the bird was immediately visible in its very large cage. On the cage was a sign which read 'My name's Charlie'. The promoter laughed at this and told me, 'That's what I call my wig', and much to the astonishment of the other customers illustrated the fact with a flourish.

The people of New Zealand were really nice and friendly to me. I was invited into their homes and always made to feel welcome. The only problem was the lack of time. I dashed from one interview to the next, from one area to another. It was hard work.

The tour was well attended and the audiences receptive, kind and considerate. My messages flowed freely and any worries I may have had about this vanished the moment I stood before a capacity crowd in Auckland. My memories of New Zealand are essentially happy ones. It is a beautiful land of glorious green with azure skies, drifting clouds, and a sense of serenity somehow reminiscent of England.

But that England is a dream recalled from a time before motorways and Motown. New Zealand will forever remain one of my favourite places on earth. It is a land of peace. I hope to return one day, and the next time I won't be so rushed. That tour physically drained me.

Michael acted as my manager and agent for two years. I enjoyed every theatre we played together, he was always a delight to be with. Eventually, though, we had to part professionally. Business was not good, but Michael and myself believed this to be mainly due to the extremely strong competition, the two Dorises had the circuit sewn up. All the prestige venues had one of the two booked and there was simply no way in. So, with regret, and with very many happy memories of a fine and funny man who was blessed with a heart of gold, the famous Michael Vine and I parted company. I still speak to Michael, he sends me a card at Christmas, and when I last contacted him, he told me that he was certain the time for my success was now. He should know, he spent a full series on the panel of *New Faces*.

Whilst appearing before a sell-out audience at one of my

favourite theatres, The Key in Peterborough, I happened to mention to the manager that I was in need of an agent. 'My friend is an agent', he said, and promised to get him to phone me.

The very next day Vincent Shaw called me on the telephone at home, inviting me to go to London and discuss matters with him. The following Friday I drove down and over coffee in his office suite, he outlined his proposals. Vincent Shaw manages many big names, he tours the Sooty Show round the theatre circuit, and produces TV shows for London Weekend Television. He could, he assured me, get theatre dates and would work at getting my name into the public's mind. To this end he proposed that I undertake a celebrity sitting for one of his clients, Miss Mandy Rice-Davies.

At the time, she was once again a very big name and in the news. The film *Scandal* was in production and Mandy was over from the USA on all the chat shows. I, of course, agreed to do this on the understanding that she be permitted to decide what would be released to the press.

Some days later, Vincent phoned me and arranged a time and date for the reading. I arrived at his suite not quite knowing what to expect. Mandy Rice-Davies entered the office, smoking a cigarette. She seemed so ordinary-looking, nothing like the glamorous image I had of her. For the next thirty minutes she paced up and down that room, lighting cigarette after cigarette, never before or since have I known anyone to be so nervous of me. As soon as I spoke to her, a spirit came through. He gave his name as Peter Rachman. The content of his message to Miss Davies is a secret that I will keep forever. It startled Mandy, and what the spirit told surprised me quite a bit, too. I never got any publicity from that exercise at all, Mandy simply refused to let me tell the press and swore me to a secrecy that I cannot break. That is a great pity, for what Peter Rachman explained that day would have made headlines.

My association with Vincent Shaw took me to theatres throughout the UK. At many of these I would follow the Sooty Show, which had played in the afternoon. Quite a contrast, and one which did not always work for me. I began to become increasingly disillusioned with the whole thing. My career had stagnated and seemed to be getting nowhere at all.

This state of affairs affected not only my income, which was to a certain extent dependent upon theatre work, but also my confidence. Why, I wondered, was I not succeeding?

At this time, I was invited by Granada TV to appear on a late night discussion show called *Up-Front*. Tony Wilson and Lucy Meacock hosted, and I was asked onto the programme to answer questions on the ethics of spiritualism and my work as a medium/psychic. Some of the questioners were incredibly rude. The way many people speak to me, at times, creates within me a feeling of something other than compassion. I always try to answer honestly, with the truth as I perceive it. Of course, this truth will not please everyone, it is, however, my personal belief. On the occasion of this show, one particular questioner, a reverend gentleman, put some very unpleasant suggestions to me. I often wonder if such people would consider asking ministers of other religions if they were agents of the devil. I am certain the Imams of the local mosques would not welcome such 'constructive' comments.

Having undergone a severe grilling in front of perhaps a million or more viewers, I was invited to join the other guests for refreshments. Imagine my surprise when the very vicar who had been branding me a satanist asked if I could give him a psychic reading. I will not elucidate on the response he received, other than to state that it was in the active negative.

I had plenty of paid work to do, the private sittings generated some income, so I was unlikely to starve, but after some years on the theatre circuit, I was still skint. It was a good job I had my mother to look after me, yet it hardly seemed fair to accept so much help from a lady who had struggled all her life.

My brothers and sisters had all made successful lives for themselves. Mike, the oldest, was a top comedian touring with the biggest names in the country. One of my sisters was a policewoman, another owned a kitchen firm, fitting top quality units. The other sister, Kathleen, was a teacher in the Salvation

Army. I, on the other hand, was getting nowhere fast.

My spirit healing clinic flourished, people came from near and far to receive the benefits of my gift. Yet I continued to attract controversy. The local press often contained letters complaining about my work. It amazes me why people take time to criticise me for doing what I think is good, you would think I was ripping my clients off for a fortune. As it was, and is, I have never asked for a penny in payment for healing.

Most of the arguments against me seem based on the fact that my healing was done through the power of God and not specifically through Jesus Christ and the established church. No one considers the fact that this healing actually works, that the sick are cured and the suffering eased from their pain. The only thing my critics seemed to be interested in was banging the Christian drum. 'By their fruit shall ye know them' says the Bible, and surely mine was good.

I am only doing right as I see it. That in itself is a Christian thing to do. It certainly has never done anyone any harm that I know of.

Birmingham Central Television invited me onto a programme called *Central Weekend Live*. The format was similar to *Up-Front*. This show was designed to examine the veracity of the late Doris Stokes who had only recently passed on. As one of the country's most prominent mediums I was asked to comment. For my troubles I received a verbal battering, especially from a rather plump disc jockey who had been a friend of Britain's former leading medium.

This particular disc jockey, in front of perhaps a million or so viewers, proceeded to vilify me. I had never clapped eyes on this Birmingham record spinner in my life, and was shocked to hear him call me, 'a third-rate mind reader'. At the interval, the producer came to me and suggested I fight back. I was simply too stunned by this unwarranted attack. I thought we were there to remember a fine and very gifted medium, not to sacrifice new ones.

After the show, in the refreshment room, this disc jockey came to me with some silly idea that I might like to be featured with him on a radio programme. Without wishing to seem aggressive, I advised him of my feelings in relation to his unprovoked assault on a man he did not know and had, before that evening, never met. I might as well have been talking to the wall, he was probably deaf from a lifetime spinning the top twenty.

When I left the television studio late that night, I found to my utter dismay that some hooligans had smashed every single window in my car. It was raining, windy, very dark and a hundred miles away from Bolton.

When I got home, I was frozen to the bone, soaking, dripping wet and extremely tired. All that, and I had achieved nothing, nothing whatsoever. I was ill in bed for the next two days after that horrible and insulting experience.

My mother could hardly believe it when I told her what had happened. But, like the good friend she has always been, she brought me tea, sympathy and all the loving care I needed to pick myself up once again.

There were no positive spin-offs from my television appearances. People did say they had seen me, but thought my involvement in such argumentative programmes did nothing to help. However, TV producers knew my name. Some time later, when Granada were producing a TV series on the paranormal, I was an obvious choice.

James Randi, Psychic Investigator featured this well-known sceptic pulling apart mediums and supernatural occurrences. He branded them all as merely fraudulent. However, the real fraud was old Randi himself. In the studio he invited his guest mediums, myself included, to pass messages to an invited audience. This was being filmed for editing at a later date. As each medium began to pass messages, which were being accepted, the incredibly rude Randi would intervene and stop the filming.

I recall that Stephen O'Brien, whom I consider to be in the top rank of British mediums, gave a very precise message indeed. The contents of this message were most certainly beyond his knowledge, yet James Randi cut this completely from the final production. It was nothing more than a total and utter farce. Then, this arrogant little man had the audacity to accuse me of being a cheat! There and then I challenged him to prove this insult to be the truth, but he just shrugged his shoulders and walked off the set. When Randi's ready – so am I.

My media profile continued to build, I had been a guest many times on local BBC and independent radio stations. Often, I would startle the presenters with the accuracy of my psychic powers.

I recall an invitation to BBC Radio Leeds for an interview with Kathrine Apanavitch, prior to appearing at the Leeds City Varieties Theatre. This rather forward young lady announced to her thousands of listeners that, as far as she was concerned, all mediums were little more than talented tricksters. A challenge indeed, and one she instantly regretted. I asked the untamed Kathrine if she would like me to give her a reading live on air. She had to agree, after all she didn't believe I could do it, and had informed her audience accordingly.

The first part of her message caused young Miss Apanavitch to gesture wildly me in an attempt to make me stop. It concerned the health of a member of her family and half of Leeds heard me give to her the incontrovertible proof. Of course, I stopped speaking as soon as she asked me, the message was obviously embarrassing and causing her anguish, something I would never ever willingly do to anyone, even Miss Apanavitch. I did, though, tell the listeners that this modern madam had excused herself on personal grounds.

However, before the end of the interview I became aware that she was going to leave BBC Leeds and return to her previous work in TV. Kathrine Apanavitch had been a member of the *EastEnders* cast, playing the girlfriend of Simon Wicks and Dirty Den. I told her then, live on air, that she was leaving her present occupation in March, and that she would become very well known on TV. This caused Miss Apanavitch to deride me as a practitioner of guesswork who had now got it all totally wrong. I remember feeling highly insulted by her hyper-critical antagonism but, in a situation like that, on radio, you are under the control of whoever is presenting the show. I obviously cannot prove my predictions at the time I make them, yet, because the spirits tell me, I personally believe them to be true. Kathrine Apanavitch laughed at me.

Some time, later whilst at BBC North to be interviewed by Bob Roberts on *The Late Show*, his producer approached me. 'I remember you, James Byrne', he said, 'I was producing at BBC Leeds when you told Miss Apanavitch that she was leaving in March. Did you know this actually happened?' Well, it didn't surprise me, the spirits have never yet told me lies.

Whilst watching TV some time later, I saw my aggressive interviewer on a game show hosted by Tom O'Connor. Kathrine Apanavitch had returned to her previous occupation, on television, just as I had predicted.

I frequently astound the press who are often cynical, red-brick-university, bought-the-T-shirt types. Many simply cannot understand my psychic powers, which are beyond reasoned scientific argument. Always I would offer, as I still do, to give nominated members of the local reporting staff psychic readings. The idea being that as I am always likely to produce factual evidence of life after death, they would then report this in their respective newspapers. This would generate interest and I would benefit from full houses in the theatres.

One particularly successful reading I gave was for a press reporter from the *Peterborough Evening Telegraph*. This nice young lady treated me with great respect, it was a very pleasant change. Carolyn Waudby responded most positively to my extremely accurate psychic message. As she approached me, I could see quite clearly, standing beside her, two old ladies. These ladies told me that they were her grandmothers and were there to give her a message of love and hope from all her family in the next world, who were watching over her. Carolyn was astounded with the detail I was able to give her and she gave me a really positive report in the paper detailing the content of the psychic message I had passed to her. A very nice and intelligent young woman, Carolyn Waudby, not too proud to accept that in this world there are things beyond the reasoning of mankind.

Despite every one of my attempts – all the press, all the TV, all the radio, I made no constructive progress at all. Months passed, and I got little or no theatre work. I just could not understand why this should be.

Vincent Shaw assured me that the real problem was the severe recession affecting the whole of the country. I could obviously see clear evidence of that, shows were folding after a few dates of a planned UK tour, due to poor advance ticket sales. Yet I knew, deep inside, that for me it was much more than the recession.

During one particularly bleak period, I sat watching TV with my mum. Thirty-seven years old and still at home with mother, what on earth was I doing with my life? I wondered, then, which way to turn. The last theatre dates I had done were over three months ago and I had next to nothing lined up for the immediate future. I was living from day to day, scratching pocket money from private readings.

Then, as I sat watching a documentary on TV about an old 'sixties hero of mine, pop singer PJ Proby, who was making a comeback attempt, I saw on screen a man called John Sutton. I watched in amazement, wondering how it could be possible for PJ Proby to be back in the public eye. I knew that this one-time superstar was a notorious riot of a man. Yet there he was on Network TV, singing and strumming a guitar like he'd never been gone. All this was thanks to his manager, John Sutton. A spirit voice whispered to me, 'Go find this man, he will lead you to success'. This ran through my mind like an electric shock, all my psychic senses told me this was important, very important.

I watched intently as the documentary continued with John Sutton telling how he had rescued PJ Proby from oblivion. If he can do it for him, he can do it for me, I thought, and heeding my spirit guides' advice, I set off to find the man who had resurrected PJ Proby.

In my heart I knew it was destiny, a power far beyond my

comprehension had directed me towards that man. There was a strange sense of determination in the way he spoke, a 'British Bulldog' grit about his demeanour, that I knew would equal achievement. I sensed that he would be the right man to manage me. He just seemed so certain of himself.

It was a difficult phone call to make. Imagine ringing someone up and telling them the spirits had told you to do it. I thought he might think I was some kind of nut. John Sutton listened to me as I told him basically what I did and what I required, i.e. a personal manager. I told him then that what I had in mind was an agreement similar to that which had led Presley to fame and fortune. I wanted John Sutton to be my Colonel Tom Parker, and all my instincts told me this was right. We agreed to meet. As I recall John said something like, 'Well, you can't be as difficult as my other performer, you don't split your trousers on stage, do you!'

7

Devil Worshipper!

Arriving at John Sutton's home in Leyland, Lancashire, on a warm August afternoon in 1991, not quite knowing what to expect, I was pleasantly surprised. His bungalow was situated in a quiet residential estate with a pleasing aspect, overlooking a tree-hung pond with mallard ducks dipping in the shaded cool. My psychic sensitivity told me that this was a happy place, it felt right and as I knocked on the door a sense of calm overcame me. It was as if I had been lost in a strange struggle with life and had found the pathway at last.

John greeted me with a healthy handshake, a warm smile and a constructive attitude. Sitting in his comfortable lounge, drinking tea and discussing psychic powers with a total stranger did not seem to phase him at all. In fact John was totally at ease about the subject. This did surprise me a little, as most people are quite shocked when you tell them you are able to receive messages and visions from the next world.

During this initial meeting I discovered why John was able to accept without question the concepts I caused him to consider. It seemed that some weeks prior to our meeting he had been advised that I was coming by another medium. John told me this incredible story: 'In early 1991 a close friend of mine went to The Gambia in Africa for a holiday. During his weeks there, this man decided to take part in a short safari into the jungle. Not hunting or anything dramatic, just a journey into the back of nowhere. Whilst out in the wilds, the safari visited a primitive village and there my friend was offered a mystical reading from the local witch doctor. The messages he received from this African included a warning about one of his friends in England. The witch doctor told him about "a man in your homeland who has only one leg, warn him, tell him the spirits have news for him. He must go and see a medium".

'This was all thousands of miles from England and on his return my friend, who is really a very down to earth type, told me of this message over a few beers in a Preston Pub. It took me a while to bring myself to actually do it, but one day, after some consideration, I decided to give it a try. But where do you go to see a medium. I didn't think "Good Old Yellow Pages" was the place, so I thumbed through a local free newspaper and, under personal services, found a small advertisement offering psychic readings from a medium called Joan. On instinct, I picked up the phone and booked an appointment.

'Joan Winfield lived in Westhoughton, near Bolton, and when I called to see her, she immediately gave me an extremely strange look. I do realise that with one leg and a grizzled pugnacious physiognomy I cut a queer character, but Joan did seem somewhat uneasy beyond the normal reaction. Handing me a pack of playing cards, she requested that I shuffle these and select a certain number.

'"There is a man coming to see you," she said, "and when this man calls, he will ask you to manage him. You've written a book", she said holding out empty hands, "this book will make you very famous, you're on TV, on the radio, in the newspapers all over the world". Joan was by this time giving me a real eyeballing. "Who are you?" she asked, "What on earth do you do? In all the years I have been giving psychic readings, I have rarely experienced one like this. You are one determined man, awkward, difficult and destined to be very, very famous. There are lights all about you."

'Mrs Winfield had absolutely no idea who I was, and I certainly did not expect to be internationally famous. The best I had hoped for in my future was selling the compact discs of PJ Proby and getting a book published about his crazy life. This

I put to Joan who, without equivocation refuted the idea. "You will never work with Proby again, that is finished. The man that is coming to you will be internationally famous. You are going to make him famous."

'That was quite a reading, considering I had never even been to see a psychic before. It seemed to startle Joan Winfield, who told me such readings were very rare. "Most people lead ordinary lives, so there is often not a lot to tell, but you are something else!"'

Having heard this from John Sutton, I could understand why he was so unperturbed about the idea that I was a theatrical stage medium. He had been expecting me, at least expecting someone, so my account of psychic powers and supernatural experiences just triggered off his entrepreneurial energies. I could almost hear his mind ticking over. 'Tell me about your career to date', he said, sipping black coffee from a personalised pot.

As I spoke, listing what I considered to be achievements, John made notes, clearly considering the points I made. The more I said about my professional life, the more I realised that it had lacked direction. The television appearances had resulted in nothing positive at all. I had been rapidly going nowhere fast. Most of my work had no discernible pattern to it, I had sold out a venue here, then never returned, created headline news in one area and failed to capitalise with theatre bookings. As we talked, I began to see that the success I sought required planning. To date, I had no plan, no future goal to aim for, my career had no strategy.

I suggested to John that he come and see me work, the better to assess the potential of this proposed venture. This idea did not appeal, as I was to discover in times to come that Mr Sutton was a man of action and also, at times, rather aggressive. 'Leave it with me', he said, 'I'll sort some venues out and take it from there.' No messing about, the decision had been made.

John introduced me to his wife, Mary, with a very optimistic 'meet my new superstar' line that had the lady laughing. As John explained to Mary that he was about to launch me into the stratosphere of success, I noted a look of concern on her friendly face. 'What will you do next, Sutton?' she said, obviously amused at her husband's affirmative approach to life. 'You've got a right one here', she smiled, indicating her husband, but I knew that he could do it. I felt right about the man, he was enthusiasm personified. I'll never forget one of the first things that he said to me: 'If I can't do it, it can't be done.' But I knew that this man could do it, my spirit voices had sent me to see John Sutton for a purpose, and that purpose was to enable me to demonstrate my gift to the world.

As I drove home to Bolton on that hot summer afternoon, I felt a strange sense of excitement running through my veins. Somewhere in the world of spirits, my guide was smiling. I had turned a different corner and my life from that day would never be the same again.

I returned to John's home later the same week to discuss venues and plan for the future. I suppose John might have been a little sceptical at what I had told him, after all it isn't every day that you get someone calling round with voices from beyond the grave.

As we talked, and John was telling me his ideas for forthcoming theatre dates, I became aware of a recently past spirit presence. 'Has someone close to your wife recently died?' I asked him. He looked a little surprised and shouted to Mary, 'Come here love, James has a message for you'. The spirit voice I heard told me that his name was Joe and he wanted to tell Mary that he loved her. 'Tell her I'm sorry, I have been a fool', he said. This startled Mary who explained that her Uncle Joseph Boydell-Thomas had recently died. He had reason, she thought, for being sorry. 'He certainly was a silly man', she said. 'Tell Mary I was led up the garden path, I have been a foolish man', the spirit of Joe Thomas seemed quite distressed and I tried, as best I could, to reassure the sorry soul. It seemed to me that in his life on earth he had behaved badly and now, recognising his faults in the full light of knowledge, wanted desperately to be forgiven. John's wife accepted this message from her late uncle, she knew exactly what he meant when he told me of his foolishness.

I then received another voice, from a woman of later years who would have been perhaps in her late sixties when she passed, 'Tell Mary I can breathe now, tell her look at my legs'. This confused Mary a bit, as she couldn't place that piece of information. 'Tell her Susan has been to the hospital about her stomach, everything will be okay.' I became aware of the name Alice. 'That's my mother, she died nearly eight years ago', John's wife said, looking quite shocked with tears in her eyes as she remembered her late mother. 'My sister is called Susan and she has had trouble with her stomach.' Mary asked me to question the spirit, 'Ask her if she is with my father'. The reply was instant and in the negative. 'No, he's not with me, he's with someone else.' At this, Mary's eyes opened wide. 'You know we always wondered about my father', she said.

Then came to me three spirits who had been in the next world for some time. 'I am Kate', said the voice, 'I know Mary', but Mary did not know her, so I asked that she remember this name. Next spoke a man: 'I was called George, I am related to Mary', but once again John's wife failed to recognise the name. Then I heard a voice say, 'I am James', but Mary did not know that name either. Still, I know when I am right and told her to check with her family. I often experience this problem whilst passing messages from long dead spirits – people in this world have either no personal knowledge of the communicator or have simply forgotten. John just gave me an old-fashioned look, picked up his pen and returned to discussing our business plans.

Some days later whilst continuing our series of meetings, Mary told me that she had checked out the messages and information which I had given to her. 'My mother, in her final days, always used to say "look at my legs", which were badly ulcerated and extremely thin. The three names you gave me belong to long dead members of my family. Kate, George and James Pennington were from Wigan, they were brothers and sister on my mother's side. In their last wills and testaments, they left money to our family. James Pennington actually left a lot of money and possessions to Joseph Boydell-Thomas, the spirit you first told me about, the spirit of my late uncle. We think that these three spirits returned in anger at the foolishness of our uncle, who on his death left almost his entire estate to a cleaning woman who was no relation of his, just a hired domestic help who befriended him.'

I was pleased to receive this confirmation and, turning to my new manager, said, 'There you go, Mr Sutton, told you I was right'. To which he replied in his somewhat sardonic style, 'Great, now what about the Marine Hall at Fleetwood'.

This was to be the first venue I demonstrated at under J'Ace Management, John's company. I had presented my powers at the Marine Hall on a number of occasions in the past, and although these demonstrations had always been extremely successful they were never well attended. This booking was to prove to be no exception to the established rule.

John had booked me to appear at a number of local venues to capitalise on the collective advertising campaign he had instituted. One booking in particular caused me a great many problems. The Leisure Centre in Leyland was owned and managed by Lancashire County Council. John signed the venue for Saturday, 21 September, and it caused a local sensation.

On Friday, 13 September 1991 the biggest evening paper in Lancashire, the *Evening Post*, carried banner headlines accusing me of 'DEVIL WORSHIP'. I had been seriously criticised in the past for supposedly dabbling with the occult, but never on such a scale. It shocked me to read that people, respectable people, thought I was an agent of Satan.

The Reverend Mike Reith of St John's, Earnshaw Bridge, Leyland, said, 'It may seem like Christians are getting sweaty over an innocent event of entertainment where we have a different kind of magician. Exposure to this sort of thing is like exposure to radiation, you think it is not affecting you, but discover the damage later'.

The Reverend Adrian Argyle of Leyland Baptist Church said, 'People in the town, both Christian and non-Christian, are opposed to the show, we are particularly concerned for people who become involved in something of this nature'.

I was being publicly excoriated for my beliefs, yet no one had asked me how I felt about all this. The truth is, I felt ill when I read what people were saying about me and I wanted John to pull out of the venue. I just dislike being abused in public. He, however, would have none of that and in a strong lecture to me outlined the ground rules of our working relationship. 'You are booked to appear. If these people want to have a go, let them, I decide when and where you demonstrate, not a lot of born-again Bible bashers'.

This did surprise me somewhat, as I knew John to be a confirmed Christian of the Church of England. But I knew that day, he would stand no messing about whatsoever. When he decided to do something, one way or another, it got done.

I told my mother what they were saying about me and I think she understood the deep hurt I felt. 'Never mind, Jim', she said, 'I love you and I know you're not a Devil.' I was very upset the night they labelled me a 'Devil Worshipper'.

John phoned me the next day to say that local feeling was running high against me. It seemed that the people of Lancashire were intent on stopping this presentation, but they were faced with one very determined man. My new manager openly denounced these agitators and in the *Blackpool Evening Gazette* nailed his colours firmly to my mast. 'James Byrne takes instructions from me, his manager, not the Devil . . . and I'm not the Devil!'

With such firm control behind me I felt safe, but wondered at John's braveness, considering I had yet to do a single public demonstration for his management company. He was certainly proving to be one forceful individual. The forthcoming months showed me just how dogmatic and determined he could be. I began to realise exactly what his wife had meant when she had told me those few weeks before, 'You've got a right one here'. I undoubtedly had, and the man was one hundred percent on my side.

At 6pm on 17 September 1991 John and I met outside Fleetwood's Marine Hall. We were both a little downhearted, the pre-presentation sales of tickets had been less than encouraging despite the fact that for many years I had been conducting services at local churches on the Fylde Coast. To a certain extent this did not surprise me, as many spiritualists frowned on my stage demonstrations, believing that these should be confined to their places of spiritual worship. This, I must say, causes me some concern. People, ordinary people, need to accept that there is life after death. The message is very, very important, more important than the nature of the venue in which it is proven. My gift absolutely proves the existence of life beyond the grave, it gives people who have lost hope a reason for living, in the proven knowledge that after physical death there is a next world, the world of spirit.

The night proved once again to be less than well attended. But those that did attend received very good actual proof of an existence beyond the grave.

That evening, a young spirit boy came to me, showing quite clearly a coffin. I could see his body, smartly dressed, and inside the sombre casket were articles of youthful affection. He held these out for me to see, a teddy bear, a toy train, obviously the playthings of his short earthly life.

I gave this information out to those present and a lady told an astounded audience that this indeed was her son. She had buried this boy the previous year and in his coffin the family had placed the toys that in this life he had loved.

I was able to give her detailed information concerning her child's death, which she agreed would have been beyond my knowledge. Proof indeed that there is a world beyond. It certainly startled a few people in the Marine Hall, Fleetwood, that night.

John was less than pleased at the turnout, he had done everything right. Posters up and out in good time, leaflets distributed throughout the area, advertisements in all the local press and still there had been little response. The main point I stressed to him at this time was that at least we did not lose any money. We nearly did, though, and neither of us got paid that night.

John accepted the fact that you simply can't win them all, and proceeded with preparations for our forthcoming presentation at Leyland.

Much to our surprise, tickets for the highly publicised demonstration at the Lancashire Leisure Complex had been very slow. This caused some consternation in our camp, only seven days away from the date with just ten tickets sold. I felt certain the bad press had frightened people. After all, who, in their right mind, would go and see a 'devil worshipper'? I wouldn't.

The newspapers were full of strange accusations, linking my presentations to everything from sour milk to murder. A certain Lancashire County Councillor constructed a campaign to have me banned from the area. Councillor Brenda Joan Wilson of South Ribble told the press, 'I have had Christians and non-Christians come up to me complaining bitterly about it. From my own point of view, I object to it for two reasons. Firstly, because I am a practising Christian and secondly, because of the psychological damage it can cause to certain people. It is totally wrong and detrimental to the health of the people of this borough.'

The councillor maintained that meetings such as the forthcoming Leyland demonstration were 'against the word of God', and led to people being 'psychologically damaged to the extent that they can harm and kill themselves and others'. Not good news for James Byrne, the townsfolk were frightened stiff by the lacerating lampoonery. No doubt Brenda Wilson meant well, but then so did Matthew Hopkins, the Witchfinder General!

The night of 21 September 1991 was marred by a number of factors outside my control. The rain poured down from a grey dark Lancashire sky, dampening the prospects for a reasonable turnout. John and I had by this time resigned ourselves to accepting the inevitable, and with a cheering clap on the back, my manager guided me to his car. 'Hope you ate a hearty breakfast', he said, implying that tonight I was the condemned man. When I saw the reception committee, I certainly felt like one.

Before the entrance to Leyland's Leisure Complex stood a large group of determined Christians. At times like these, I wonder at the real motive behind such actions. There they stood, in the wind and rain, offering advice and leaflets to those intending to attend my demonstration. I understand that they want to profess their faith, but fail to comprehend how such displays of peaceful force can promote religion. They are more likely to have the opposite effect, I would think.

The anti-Byrne demo seemed to be the final deterrent. Only about 120 people attended and in very difficult circumstances I began my presentation. Rain battered down on the flat roof, causing my amplified voice to be lost in an echo of powerful precipitation.

Inside the entrance hall, a vicar preached about 'hellfire and Deuteronomy', surrounded by a swelling group of militant evangelists. The Director of Leisure for South Ribble called the police, some louts smashed the cars in the car park and I was labouring against the odds. You just can't win them all.

As we left the building at the end of a less than successful evening, we were escorted to our vehicle by the very vicar who had, but a short while before, been denouncing me as an agent of Satan. He seemed a nice, sincere man, and I believe he wished us no personal harm. His large umbrella sheltered me from the driving rain which had poured without cessation from the moment we had left John's house. Given different circumstances, I am sure we could have been friends, I feel certain he prayed for my soul that night. When I got home to Bolton I said a prayer for him and his friends. Perhaps one day my gift will be accepted by the world as being from God, for in my prayers, I always ask that it will be.

John picked up the bills for the Leyland fiasco, and once again we made no wages. I felt really very guilty about this. When I first went to see John, I had told him about the numerous sell-outs I had enjoyed at prestige venues throughout the UK, yet here I was, unable to pull a crowd big enough to cover the cost of a simple provincial promotion.

The problems and bad press didn't seem to bother my new

manager at all. No doubt he had experienced controversy before, having promoted the infamous trouser-splitting Texan, PJ Proby. One thing I did notice was the constant effort he put into projecting my name. John wrote to everyone, the TV, the newspapers, the radio, and as time passed, it began to work.

My less than positive press had created an interest in James Byrne. I hated it, the insults stung me, but through that fire of unprovoked vilification, I emerged a stronger person. More able to stand the whips and scorns of my proud oppressors who, probably from the best of motives, extended the remit of their various offices to insult me.

The very personal attacks upon my demonstrations did however continue. The councillor who had labelled me a 'devil worshipper' called on the full council to institute a total ban on James Byrne.

The motion to stop me from presenting my gift from God at future presentations in Lancashire County was, thankfully, defeated.

Brenda Wilson had pleaded her case with great eloquence, stating: 'I do not blame the council for permitting the James Byrne Promotion to proceed, as there is no directive covering this sort of situation'. Despite announcing to her fellow councillors that she 'didn't mind being laughed at' and warning that 'I will not allow the word of God to be mocked', her motion was thrown out.

When she was asked to comment on this defeat, she said, 'I might have lost the battle, but I have not lost the war'. Obviously not one to accept failure, Mrs Wilson rounded on her colleagues. 'The council has a responsibility to all the citizens of this borough and God help us all now!'

Perhaps the last word on this unseemly attack should be left with Mrs Wilson's fellow councillor, Mr Norman Crossley, who told the press that he considered the whole issue had been 'taken far too seriously'.

It is, in my opinion, a very serious thing to make the kind of statements this lady made about me. At least her own council did not agree with her, nor I suspect did many others. She has my sympathy, I too know what it is like to be a voice in the wilderness, but at least I have never used that voice to castigate others.

John Sutton had been actively promoting the positive aspects of my psychic powers to all and sundry. Then one morning in late September he phoned me with an interesting challenge. 'Listen, James, I have just spoken to the Programme Controller of Red Rose Gold Radio in Preston. I told him you could contact his deceased relatives and give him a psychic reading over the phone.' I asked my manager what the boss of this radio station intended. 'Well, when I told him what you could do, he indicated his disbelief by using a well known anglo-saxon term, commonly associated with public sporting events'. Never one to be lost for words, my manager.

When John Myers telephoned, I knew at once that this was his way of auditioning me. I had to prove to this man that I was everything my mentor had said that I was. The voices were strong and my spirits told me true. The information I gave to Mr Myers so startled him that he invited me there and then on to the station's late night phone-in to demonstrate my gift.

I contacted John Sutton with the news. 'You're going to be a star, my boy', he said, pleased that I had grasped the opportunity he had gained for me. That was what I so liked about my manager, he opened up doors to areas I had found inaccessible in previous times. This was undoubtedly due to his constant application and endeavour. I have never yet spoken to him without either being lectured on my presentation, or advised about forthcoming events, sometimes quite vehemently. But at all times he is absolutely determined, you can't really ask for more than John gives, I'm sure he dreams about success in his sleep. As he says, 'If I can't do it, it can't be done'. It was beginning to look as if he could.

Red Rose Gold Radio, Lancashire's biggest independent radio station, announced over the airwaves that on Thursday 24 October 1991 they would be broadcasting James Byrne. The protests started all over again.

I really did think that the establishment would leave me well alone having been defeated at council level. I was, however, being too optimistic. They hit the headlines all over again with plans to surround the radio station and prevent my presentation from going ahead.

'CHRISTIANS IN RADIO PSYCHIC PROTEST' said the *Lancashire Evening Post*, quoting a Pastor, David Parry, as saying 'many of my church members have asked for prayers to be said'. There was one aspect of this outrage that I, at this time, was unaware of: Red Rose Gold Radio is based in a converted church in St Paul's Square, Preston. It was undoubtedly the fact that I was about to conduct a seance on formally consecrated ground that had caused the outrage, which was at this time breaking around my head.

The *Daily Star* carried a strange story which purported to outline the content of my broadcast which was scheduled for that evening. 'WRINKLIES RAVE FROM THE GRAVE' it said, suggesting that I was going to make contact with the spirits of dead rock and roll stars, such as Buddy Holly or John Lennon.

How I was supposed to do that was beyond me! I can think of no reason why people I have no connection with, be they pop singers, film stars or anyone else, should try and contact me. There would simply be no reason for them to speak to me and I am sure that playing their earthly recordings on air would make no difference to them whatsoever. It would be much like you answering the telephone to find Michael Jackson at the other end, wanting to pass the time of day with you, because you had his *Bad* album on the stereo. Why would he do that? He just wouldn't, would he? That is a plain truth. He might just phone your number if his sister was visiting you. Then he would have a reason to call, but without that reason, that connection, neither Michael Jackson in body, nor Buddy Holly in spirit would make that call.

That is why I laugh when I read about such and such a medium speaking with Elvis. Why, you must ask yourself, would he want to do that? The answer is quite obvious, he simply wouldn't, it's just a very good story for the tabloids to tell to impress the gullible. I am a medium, a real medium, and

I personally doubt the veracity of these claims.

As we drew into Red Rose Gold Radio's car park, I could see a large group of people gathered at the front gates. They were singing a hymn, 'The Old Rugged Cross', I think. It was a cool dark night with a promise of rain in the chill October air. Surely these people had something better to do with their time than this, I thought. John popped over to speak to the crowd. 'Sing us "There is a Green Hill Far Away", I like that one', he said. They didn't, nor did they smile, but I had to at the sheer audacity of this man I called manager. As we entered the once consecrated church housing Red Rose Gold and *The Tony Newman Phone-in*, I began to feel slightly ill at ease.

That night I was about to become the United Kingdom's first radio psychic, and Tony Newman, along with many thousands of others, would hopefully be astounded at the evidence I was attempting to pass. I would be trying to prove, beyond any reasonable doubt, that life, despite physical death, continues.

A new chapter in my life as a medium had opened. It was to prove to be an exciting, if sometimes traumatic one. As John and I sat behind the microphones looking across at Tony Newman, neither of us knew for certain what would happen next.

8

On The Radio

Few people can imagine what it is like being asked to prove one's psychic gift live on the radio, the stress is tremendous. Consider my position: I am seated in a studio, deep inside a building housing the station. Certainly, I cannot see the callers phoning in, the only contact I do have is through the microphones and headsets linked to the telephone system. Added to this, the presenters are always willing to 'have a go' at me, and Red Rose Gold's Tony Newman was no exception.

Tony began this particular evening by questioning me about my beliefs. The truth is very easy for me to tell and, as always, I explained briefly the ethos of my spiritualist religion. Of course, I understand that everyone will not agree with me, even some of my fellow spiritualists find fault with the public demonstrations which I give. Soon I was taking flak from the callers, and one gentleman called Alan gave me a real ear bashing, 'I am a spiritualist, I have met you . . . the side that you put over puts spiritualism on a showman level . . . you should speak about the other side . . . not the messages . . . as I've seen you on TV . . . all you're saying is, I can prove, I can prove. You don't tell them about spiritualism as a proper religion . . . the prayer and healing which helps people . . . you also never thank your spirit guides . . . Consider the four points of the cross, love, compassion, mercy and understanding . . . tell people about that and they can't criticise you'.

Obviously, Alan had never faced a hostile audience of

sceptics. They only accept proof, and sometimes not even that. Mere generalisations, however profound and true they may be, would prove unacceptable. To offer the public a lecture on the essence and ethics of spiritualism might even result in a walk-out. It would certainly not constitute a reasonably entertaining and informative radio programme. Yet some of my friends in the spiritualist religion refuse to accept this as being the blunt truth. In fact, wherever I go, I find that some of my severest critics are often practising spiritualists themselves. Perhaps they hate the idea that I demonstrate in theatres, I have been condemned for being far too 'showbiz'. Some spiritualists find fault with the whole idea of publicly presenting psychic powers, and this really hurts me at times, to think these people who are supposedly on my side offer me public criticism. I sincerely believe that the more people who come to accept the truth of life after death, the better it is for humanity. It is the fear of oblivion which frightens people, and my public demonstrations hopefully ease that fear.

Most callers ringing the *Tony Newman Phone-In* wanted me to give them messages from the next world. This is something that I always try, and generally succeed to do. The next person ringing Red Rose Gold was a young lady with a trembling voice. Tony introduced her, 'Jenny, you're through to James Byrne'. This woman sounded quite emotional as she explained her feelings to me. 'I went tingly all over as the programme came on, I've never ever been to a spiritualist before, I wanted to, but . . .'. Her voice faltered as she sought the words to express her meaning. Listening to this lady fumble with the story of her search for truth, I became aware of a spirit, it was the spirit of her late father. Jenny continued, 'I keep going cold all over . . . I think I know who it is'.

The voice of Jenny's late father spoke to me of personal tragedy in his daughter's young life. I advised her then, as I advise all who seek my help, 'Tell me nothing, we must confirm that the spirit is who he tells me he is. We can only do this by you acknowledging that the information I give is correct. Do not be afraid to tell me if I am wrong, we both need to verify the truth of this matter. Only by proving their identity, through passing such information, can both you and I be certain that the message is from a spirit which is known to you. Once we can do this, then you can accept the message as being correct.'

Having established the ground rules, I began to pass on the information I was receiving from the spirit world. 'Your father has been gone quite a while.'

'That's true.'

'This man suffered a great deal before he passed away.'

'Yes. He suffered mainly in his chest area.'

'That is right. He keeps telling me that one of his main difficulties before he passed away was with his breathing, I don't mean in the last five minutes of his life, he was very bad with his breathing for some time before he died. On top of that, this man lost quite a bit of weight.'

'That is absolutely true.'

'Tell me, have you got a brother?'

'I have two brothers.'

'Yes, but has one of these been out of your life for some time, the spirit says, one of your brothers has not been there for a long time, does that make sense to you?'

'Yes, it certainly does.'

'This man also says that your new place is very nice, have you just moved house?'

'Yes, that's right, that's true.'

Sometimes, things come through in messages which are very personal, and it is absolutely impossible to tell someone live on air, with many thousands of people listening, the extremely private details of their lives which are given to me by the communicating spirit. So I have got to be very tactful. Jenny's father had told me just such extremely delicate information about his daughter. I tried, as best I could, to convey the gist without distressing this obviously emotional young lady.

'Your father tells me that the last two years of your life have been the worst you have ever experienced.'

'Yes, that's true.'

'He says he's sick of seeing his daughter upset all of the time, he tells me that there have been tears, anxiety, he says you've been so very frightened. I don't know what you have been frightened of, Jenny, but he says somebody has got a lot to answer for.'

'You're absolutely correct.'

'I think you know who he means. Have you ever lost a baby?'

'Yes, I have, two.'

'Your father has got one of these children with him. I know this is a common name and all my critics will jump on me, but were you very close to someone called John, you were very close to this John.'

'That is my father's name.'

At this point, having proven beyond reasonable doubt that the spirit speaking to me was indeed the father of Jenny, I felt able to pass her his message of hope for the future.

'Your father tells me you were recently divorced.'

'That is very true.'

'He said to tell you that the greatest happiness in your life is yet to come, in fact, it hasn't even begun yet, so come on, Jenny, give me a smile. Being a psychic, I can see it you know.'

I am certain that message helped this young lady, it contained verifiable proof of identity and offered her hope for the future. The fact that this message was passed over the airwaves seemed, to me at least, to be absolutely irrelevant. For Jenny, it was surely a comfort, knowing that the father she had loved watches over her from the world of spirit.

Giving ordinary people hope, no matter where or how I do it, means a lot. It is, I am certain, one of the reasons God gave this gift to me. To all those who ridicule me for being showbusiness and theatrical, I can say only this, listen to the messages, they are the truth, they are the reason I continue, for without my mediumship the spirits would perhaps be unable to offer the love, consolation and joy those messages bring.

For three hours that night, I answered the questions Tony Newman and the callers put to me. Most of those phoning in wanted me to give them information from their departed loved ones. They sought reassurance that beyond the grave there was indeed life after death. The pressure and stress were extremely intense. On reflection, I wonder how on earth I did it. John kept the black coffee coming, and occasionally passed me scribbled notes which made me laugh and eased the tension considerably. I won't go into great details, but some of his written suggestions on what to say in response to Mr Newman's jibes would have required a contortionist to undertake them. They most certainly would have got me banned from Red Rose and every other radio station forever. I had absolutely no intention of repeating such ideas on air. Though we did laugh about them at the time.

Before we left the studios that night, Tony Newman asked me if I could give him a message for the future. The strain of having just undertaken three solid hours of psychic reading over the airwaves had tired me a great deal, but looking across at him I sensed a man whose life was about to change. He did not believe me when I told him then that his future was not to be with Red Rose Gold. For on that night, I told Tony Newman that he would be travelling overseas and in the future he would be a big name in both Europe and the United Kingdom. It was to be many, many months later when this occurred. In fact, Tony Newman went overseas to Vienna to work with a major radio station in Europe.

The following night, we were in the news again, 'CHRISTIANS PROTEST AT PSYCHIC'S PHONE-IN', said the headlines in the *Lancashire Evening Post*. It didn't stop John Myers, the Director of Programmes, from expressing his great delight at the success of our presentation. 'The phones were jammed solid for four hours and for every protest call, there was another one interested in what James Byrne had got to say.'

Despite the controversy, we were invited back to Red Rose Gold Radio. John Myers explained why: 'There were a lot of people who were shocked and surprised at how good he was', he told the *Lancashire Evening Post*. Reason enough to encourage Red Rose Gold Radio to continue with the United Kingdom's first-ever psychic phone-in. Not that things would run smoothly from that point, the establishment does not quit that easily.

The Reverend Andrew Parkinson, in a sermon to his parishioners at St Christopher's Church, Lea, Preston, told his congregation not to listen to the broadcast from the radio station which was featuring James Byrne. This did not please Mr Myers, who said to the *Evening Post*, 'We accept that any vicar has the right to question what we might do, and ask his congregation to think about it. But to pulpit bash and tell them not to listen to us, is not on.'

Red Rose Gold had sought special permission from the Independent Broadcasting Authority for the programmes featuring my spiritual messages. So for a local vicar to say such inflammatory things seemed a little out of order, at least to me and John Myers. When asked for his comments, the Bishop of Blackburn distanced himself from the argument by telling the press, 'a Bishop has no control over what individual vicars preach about'. Obviously a very diplomatic man.

My career as a stage medium continued to progress, if a little slowly at times. I gained most of my personal income from private readings, much as I had been doing for the previous eight or nine years. People would come back to me for guidance or counselling on an almost regular basis. My personal following in and around Lancashire had developed considerably. It was fortunate that I was able to earn money this way, I certainly never earned a single penny from the radio broadcasts I made. I did not even get paid for my expenses. This fact seemed to astound many of my friends. People would say to me, you must be making a fortune now, James, we hear you on the radio all the time. Nothing could have been further from the truth. In fact, those presentations at Red Rose Gold cost me money. I had to reply to hundreds and hundreds of letters, all at my own expense.

However, some of those letters did not receive a reply, for some simply did not warrant it. One woman wrote stating that when she had been put through to me live on air, she had been so astounded at my accuracy that she had said, no, no, no, to everything I said. In her letter, she asked if it was possible for me to give her a private reading, as she had been absolutely amazed and shocked. It seems that this lady was under the impression that I was a charlatan, and on receiving proof of my veracity, had been unable to respond. You can imagine how I feel about getting a letter such as that. Presenters like Tony Newman look at me as if I am totally stupid when that happens, and what can I say to a caller who tells me on air that the information I am giving them is absolutely, totally wrong. I know what I am hearing, yet they are denying the truth.

It makes me look a complete idiot. So when I do receive letters such as that, and I receive them quite often, I always say a little prayer of thanks to my spirit guides, then I file them in an appropriate place.

One of my regular clients, Sandra Bateson of Horwich, near Bolton, first came to me nearly ten years ago. I will never forget this young lady, who came in a distressed condition following the death of her husband, Robert. I can vividly recall telling her the exact details of his death – he had been involved in a road traffic accident. As Sandra sat in my home, I saw quite clearly the events surrounding her late husband, and his untimely demise. The place where the road traffic accident took place came to me as a vision which played in front of my eyes. I recounted this to Sandra as she sat softly weeping on the settee in our living room in Bolton. I had to call for my mother to make her a cup of tea. These were not tears of distress, but tears of absolute joy, in the certain knowledge that her husband, whom she had dearly loved, lived on in the world of spirit.

The life of Sandra Bateson was clearly mapped out for me to see. I could see signposted quite plainly the major events which were about to take place in her immediate future. Her late husband told me many, many personal details about this lady, and asked to me to guide her through the problems which would lay ahead of his wife.

Obviously I cannot disclose the confidential nature of the messages he gave me from the world beyond, but Sandra has, over the years, been able to confirm the absolute accuracy of the detailed evidence her late husband has passed.

Both she and her relatives frequently visit my home in Bolton. Some five years following the death of her husband, Sandra and her mother came to see me together. This was following the death of her father. Whilst Sandra and her obviously distressed parent were seated in my living room, I became aware of the man who had recently died. I could see that this man had passed away in a room in a house belonging to the lady before me. The clarity of my vision, which I described in great detail, surprised Sandra's mother who, up to this time, had disbelieved her daughter's accounts of my accuracy. On this occasion, I recall telling Sandra that on her father's coffin she had placed a single rose. I was shown a rose by the spirit, he showed me that on this was attached a card and it said, 'lots of love, Jennifer'. This meant nothing to me, but when I told Sandra what the card said, she broke down in floods of uncontrollable tears. 'My father always called me Jennifer for a joke, it was his pet name for me. No one, not even my mother knew that, and when he died she questioned why I had written, "lots of love, Jennifer". No one could have known that, it was our little secret.' That information certainly surprised both Sandra and her mother, especially her mother.

Over the years, I have continued to see Sandra Bateson and, I believe, I have helped that lady through some very difficult times in her life. I have most definitely been able to predict with some degree of certainty the exact nature of many of her personal and private relationships.

I meet many people as a medium. People from all walks of life, often seeking help and guidance, or just reassurance, following the death of a loved one. Others have social problems, personal tragedies linked to the complexities of life in this modern material world. Some years ago, one such man who sought help called at my home late one Sunday afternoon. He had been drinking heavily.

At the time he was, he said, undergoing an extremely traumatic period in his life. I was able to advise and guide that man through the help of his spirit communicator, who told me that in the years to come this man would be happier than at any time before. His late father spoke to me of the good works his son, now a drunken ruin, would eventually do.

As I explained this to him, he seemed to brighten a little. The tears of emotion ceased and I could sense a change in his ravaged demeanour. 'Your father tells me that in the immediate future you will find a solution to your problems. The answer is right in front of you, he says that you're going to be a teacher'. The look of hope that flashed across his face reminded me of the joy my messages can bring to people floundering in a sea of despair.

As he was leaving my home the young man turned to thank me. 'You've given me something to look forward to', he said, shaking my hand. 'I intend to try and start again, just like you said.' With that, he walked purposefully out of my life forever.

It is strange to me now, after all these years have passed, that this very man, who has now come to terms with his life, criticises me for being a medium. For he became a born-again Christian, and was employed by the local authority, teaching adults with disabilities. His life is now both rewarding and fulfilled, yet he has nothing but vilification to heap upon me, a man he once turned to for help. What can I say? I am only pleased that a lost soul has been saved.

Many people ask me if it is possible for members of non-English-speaking groups to receive messages from the spirit world. The answer to that is yes. In fact, certain friends of mine are non-English-speaking Chinese. These very nice people attend my home for readings as a family group. The main problem in conducting the readings is that only one of the group speaks English. This creates some delay whilst I am communicating with their deceased relatives in the next world. I repeat what the spirits say to me and the English-speaking member translates it into Chinese. It takes ages.

I can understand that the question is, how on earth can I understand Chinese, being a boy from Bolton. The truth of the matter is that I simply can't understand Chinese, but the spirits communicate with me in a language that I can comprehend. This information or message I pass to the individual who can understand the language which I speak, Bolton English. The Chinese spirit people who come through to me often pass messages concerning their homeland. They are obviously able to interpret their language and communicate with me in such a way that I will be able to understand, and the contents of their messages are very similar to those which I pass to every other individual or group that I meet. The fact that these people do not speak English makes no difference whatsoever. Their relatives in the spirit world wish them love and affection, the same as the relatives and loved ones of any people wish their relations here on earth. In the matter of language, there is absolutely no difference whatsoever in the spirits' ability to communicate.

I find that religious barriers do not exist in the world of spirit. These barriers are simply inventions of human beings living in a material world. For in the next world, the world of spirit, there simply is no barrier whatsoever. The only barrier is truth. For it is truth which is the rule of law in the world of spirit. Religion and belief in this life mean little, or nothing, in the next world. It is the way we have conducted our lives that counts for everything. The fact that we have presented ourselves in a nominated house of religion each Saturday or Sunday counts for absolutely nothing, if during the rest of the time we have behaved in a anti-social, aggressive or ungodly manner. What really counts in the next life is the law of cause of effect: if in this world you have behaved in a wicked way, then you must obviously expect that in the next life you will be called to account. It matters not whether you are Hindustani, Muslim, Pakistani, Jew, Catholic, whatever your religion or ethnic origin, in the world beyond you are faced with the truth. If, in this existence, your behaviour has been unacceptable, then in the next world it will be equally unacceptable, except that you will then understand the true nature of your actions. Believe me, to each action there is a reaction, i.e. a cause and an effect. We create our own heaven and prepare our own hell.

The response to my radio presentation at Red Rose Gold in Preston had been quite phenomenal. Both John Myers and

Tony Newman told me that the station was inundated with calls asking for more. The public had obviously enjoyed the experience. However, both Tony and John considered that what I was doing required some form of proof, and both had made several uncomplimentary comments on the shows they presented, suggesting that my psychic readings were little more than an elaborate charade.

It is obviously very difficult to prove to every single person that my gift is a genuine one. How, without individually speaking to each listener, could I convince the general public that my psychic powers were for real and not simply a very clever trick? I was often accused of being a magician. No one could explain quite how this alleged gimmick worked, but nonetheless, opted for the idea that all I did was a clever con.

This problem was, to a great extent, solved by an idea presented to me by my manager, John Sutton. We were both somewhat affronted by the extremely sceptical nature of much of the approach made to us by both callers and presenters in the media. John, having toured the country with me on various presentations in theatres and halls, had noted an increasing amount of psychic phenomena occurring around my person. In one venue close to Preston, ghostly footsteps had walked down the centre aisle of the auditorium and disappeared on reaching the stage. The entire audience heard these, much to their astonishment. At another venue in St Helens, an extremely loud banging noise became evident during one of my demonstrations. It sounded almost as if the walls were being beaten down by invisible hands. This continued for approximately 30 seconds to the amazement of those in the theatre.

At a venue near Birmingham, whilst speaking to the audience, we all became aware of voices transmitting through the loudspeaker system. I immediately ceased speaking and listened to these voices, which seemed to be coming from the next room. Whilst I am demonstrating my gift in public I find it extremely distracting to be spoken over by the audience or other sources. It is almost impossible for me to work under such conditions. I therefore suggested to the stewards in the theatre that we open the door leading to the next room, which was a public bar belonging to the theatre, and ask the people to be quiet. This we did, and to the absolute astonishment of the audience, when the door was unlocked, we found that the room was entirely empty and in darkness. In fact, as soon as these doors were opened the mysterious voices ceased entirely. The stewards gave me some very strange looks, I can tell you.

It seemed that my powers were increasing gradually, and that the spirits were now able to communicate through me almost directly to those in my immediate presence. In discussions with my manager, I suggested that this phenomenon would possibly work to our advantage, by enabling me to prove to a wider public that my psychic gift was a genuine one. The problem was how to channel this developing power and thereby enable people to experience psychic phenomena for themselves. John suggested an experiment: 'Project your powers over the airwaves, the listeners can ring the radio station and tell everyone what happens', he said, with one of those manic glints in his eyes.

The idea had a certain appeal. More people would get a chance to undertake a psychic experience, thereby proving my gift. For how could this situation be rigged? We would have no control over who would phone in, the listeners themselves and the radio switchboard would decide who I would speak to.

'We'll do it', I said, 'but it had better work or I'll look a right fool'. John just laughed, slapped me on the back and with his usual forcefulness explained that I could not fail. 'If I say this will succeed, then believe me, it will.' All we had to do was convince the programme controller of Red Rose Gold to let us have a go. I left this entirely with my manager. After all, he did say that if he couldn't do it, it couldn't be done.

9

The Psychic Experiment

Due to the popularity of the demonstration on radio, what had been an initial guest spot turned into a series. In a meeting with John Myers, we agreed to further demonstrations on air. The format John suggested for the presentation to be broadcast on 2 December 1991 was to be slightly different. In response to the numerous challenges I had received to prove beyond doubt that my powers were real, John explained that I would project these over the airwaves in what would be the United Kingdom's first live Psychic Experiment on air. 'This will astound your listeners', he told the programme controller, 'and stop you from telling everyone that James is, in your opinion, just a gifted trickster.' The showdown was on!

For days prior to this broadcast, Red Rose Gold announced to the listeners that James Byrne would be offering a supernatural experience to the public on his forthcoming broadcast.

The night of 2 December 1991 is firmly etched in my memory. John Sutton had assured me that this was going to prove beyond any shadow of a doubt that my powers were genuine and verifiable. Tony Newman thought otherwise, and even I had my doubts. It was an experiment in every sense of the word, for neither I nor anyone else, could have predicted the outcome. John did: 'Tonight, James Byrne, you will be a sensation, the whole of Lancashire will be astounded by this demonstration'. At least he was confident, I was less than sure, the spirits respond at their own discretion, no medium can demand their attention.

In the studio, my hands began to perspire, I felt ill. What if it all failed? People would be laughing at me. No one had ever tried anything remotely like this before. Uri Geller had bent spoons and started watches, but I was attempting to conduct an instantaneous Psychic Experience in thousands of homes all at once. The fear of failure almost paralysed me, but I well recalled the words of my mentor, 'trust in the spirits'. The thought gave me strength.

Before we began the transmission, Tony Newman handed me a pile of letters. 'Read this', he said. It was a scribbled note from the switchboard operator concerning a prediction I had made on air some months earlier. 'I'm going to start the show by reading that', he said. 'Are you sure this experiment is a good idea, it will never work, you know.'

John gave him one of his 'shut up and get on with it' glares, and we were live.

Tony	Tonight, fact or fantasy, Red Rose Gold's Night of Supernatural Psychic Experience . . . Is it fact, or is it fantasy? Tonight, at 10.45pm, James Byrne will attempt to prove his psychic powers on air. He says he can transmit these over the airwaves, and I say he can't.

People wishing to take part in this experience should prepare themselves for a journey into the unknown. Write down the name of James Byrne, make sure you get it right, JAMES BYRNE, have a photograph or personal memento of the spirit you would like to contact in front of you and at the appointed time, concentrate on the written name James Byrne and look at the photograph or personal memento. IS IT FACT or IS IT FICTION? Is it hogwash or what? We will find out on this programme in the next three hours.

This psychic phenomenon cannot harm you,

these are simple messages of love channelled through James Byrne. Many will experience the feeling of being in the presence of their departed loved ones, some may even notice movement or slight changes in the photograph or treasured memento they are holding. There is no reason to be afraid, those in the next life want you to know they are watching over you and are at peace. All will be revealed in the fullness of time, so stay tuned to Red Rose Gold, a night of SUPERNATURAL EXPERIENCE, or is it a load of old hogwash, we will find out . . .

That was how Tony Newman introduced the UK's first live Psychic Experiment. My hands were really sweating now!

Tony	Good evening, James.
James	Good evening, Tony.
Tony	At our last meeting, you said to a lady called Carol that she was heavily pregnant and you predicted that she would have a baby girl and it would be born in the early part of December. We received a call from Carol herself who says she has just given birth to a bouncing baby girl on 2nd December.
James	I am very pleased to hear that.
Tony	To our listeners listening to us tonight, may we remind you that if you feel apprehensive, switch off, we have three minutes to go. James, what are you going to do in three minutes time?
James	All I want people to do out there is have some article, whether it be a piece of jewellery or a photograph, whatever, belonging to somebody that the person would like to feel the presence of, and I want them at the given time to concentrate on my name, that's all they've got to do, write my name down, just concentrate on it, the name

	James Byrne, for as long as the music lasts. Afterwards people can ring in, telling us exactly what happened, if anything did.
Tony	Write down the name of James Byrne, JAMES BYRNE.
James	That's right, then concentrate on that name whilst the music is being played, very, very strongly, and at the end of the music, do contact us and tell us of your experience if there's been any, whichever is the case. That's basically it, you see, I don't want to say what's going to happen, I want people to ring me and tell me what's happened.
Tony	Sure, okay. You say though, that it's certainly not harmful.
James	Not at all, not at all. It will be the most pleasant experience of their day.
Tony	You don't want to say what the experience will be?
James	Oh no, because I think it will be something different probably for each individual, there's no one explanation, but having said that, I don't want to put thoughts into people's heads, I would rather people ring in and say in their own words what's happened or is happening.

There was no point in my outlining the kind of experiences which individuals might expect. My critics would have labelled this, 'Auto-Suggestion', proving nothing whatsoever. What I wanted this Psychic Experiment to do was to prove, beyond reasonable doubt, that my gift was genuine; that people really could receive supernatural phenomena direct through my transmitted powers.

I looked across the table hoping to get reassurance from the man who had persuaded me that all this would work. John looked totally nonplussed by the whole affair. 'More coffee James?' he said, filling my cup from his new mauve flask. Always prepared for the shows, John brought hot black coffee wherever we went. Tonight we wouldn't require caffeine to keep us awake, the experiment would do that. Tony adjusted his headphones, gave me a disbelieving look, and proceeded to introduce the listeners to a supernatural adventure unique in radio history.

Tony   So, clear the phone lines now, if you will, that's 0772 561000, the switchboard is glowing as always, so if you'd just like to hang up, because in one minute's time, we will be leading you on a journey into the beyond.

There's no reason to be afraid, if you are afraid you can switch off the radio if you don't want to go through this experience. Those in the next life want you to know that they are watching over you and are at peace, the words of James Byrne. I say that James can't do this, James says he can. So, he's going to take a minute's concentration along with you and we will see. FIVE, FOUR, THREE, TWO, ONE – listeners, concentrate while the music plays, your minute starts NOW.

Tony played some really nice weird music, cellos and pianos tinkling to set the mood. I concentrated all my psychic powers, attempting to project these through the microphone in front of me, over the airwaves into the homes of countless thousands of listeners. I urged the spirits to help me. 'Let the power go', I said, in a silent plea to those in the next life who are my spirit guides. I could feel a strange surge of energy and became aware of a calming hand holding mine. The studio seemed somehow altered and surreal, I looked across at John and saw his face set firm, unflinching, willing me to succeed. Then, as soon as it began, it was over, and Tony was talking to me.

Tony   Well, there was your minute and I want you to call 0772 561000 and share what happened. Give us a call and we'll see the reactions, the switchboard is beginning to light up again. We will take reactions as soon as we know the first name. We also want the 'fors' and 'against' of course. If nothing happened to you, we would like to hear from you, and if something did, we would also like you to tell us exactly what did happen. So, the 'fors' and 'against', if nothing happened, give us a call, if something did happen, WHICH I DOUBT, give us a call, either way.

Okay, our first caller, Margo.

Margo	Hello.
Tony	You're through to James.
James	Hello love.
Margo	Hello James. I've just been sitting looking at your name and I have got a jug in front of me that belonged to my grandma and I could hear a voice in my head saying, 'our Margo, Margo' . . .
James	What could you actually hear. Could you hear a voice?
Margo	I could hear a voice, yes.
James	Was it a voice you knew?
Margo	Oh, definitely.
James	So it wasn't a strange experience to you then.
Margo	No. I turned round and said to my husband, 'I felt as if I was being pushed backwards and that I could see a vision in front of me and I could just hear her saying, it's our Margo, because she's Scottish and she was going, "our Margo, our Margo, our Margo". It was really strange.
James	Has it made you feel better?
Margo	Excited, I feel all fluttery.
James	I bet it's the nicest part of the day this, isn't it?
Margo	Yes.
Tony	Our next caller is Marion. Hello Marion.
Marion	Hello James.
James	Hello Marion, did you experience something?
Marion	Yes, we did experience something actually. It was a piece of jewellery that started to tick, and it had

actually stopped at roughly the time that we got the phone call from the hospital, where somebody was poorly, and it started to tick, just as Tony sort of counted down . . .

James   I take it you mean a watch, do you?

Marion   A watch, yes. It started to tick, and it had actually stopped.

James   Is it working now?

Marion   It's working now, yes. I don't believe it.

James   Well that's brilliant, love, thanks for ringing and telling me, you wouldn't believe how many people are on the phone.

Tony   Our next caller is Sandra.

Sandra   Hello James.

James   Hello Sandra.

Sandra   I've got a photograph of my brother and all I can say is, his face seemed to waver, but there was no voices, no nothing. I did not hear anything.

James   When you say his face seemed to waver, what do you mean, love. Do you mean the expression on his face?

Sandra   Yes, yes, it seemed to move.

James   Did it?

Sandra   Yes.

James   How has that made you feel?

Sandra   I don't know, funny.

James   Well, have a cup of tea and sit down.

Tony   Our next caller is through to James.

Caller   Hello.

James   Hi.

Caller   I was holding a photograph of my brother-in-law, Brian, he was killed seven weeks ago, today. When I was looking at the photo, it sort of moved, his faced moved, and then there was like a light round his face, and I could hear Brian saying, 'You know, I feel like a right idiot'. It's the kind of thing he would have said.

James	He's not on his own there, love.
Caller	It was the kind of thing he would have said, I felt so peaceful.
James	I am so glad.

Obviously, not everybody experienced a positive response to my psychic projection. Some did ring in to say that they had expected to observe phenomena, which for them did not take place. This is the problem with mediumship, it can never work for everybody all the time. If it did, then people would suspect that it was a trick, and what I do is no trick. It is the truth, and the control of that truth is beyond my power.

One lady contacted the *Tony Newman Phone-In* complaining almost, that I had failed to prove to her that there was a world beyond.

Tony	Our next caller is Jill. Hello Jill, you're through to James.
Jill	Hello James.
James	Hello Jill.
Jill	I'm afraid I didn't experience anything, and I really thought I would actually, because my mother died about four years ago, and she was a spiritualist, she firmly believed in it. She always said that she would contact me and never has done. So, I thought that really I would get a reaction from it, you know.
James	I'm really sorry to hear that, because it must be very disappointing. This is the funny thing about mediumship, sometimes it works, sometimes it doesn't, that's why I am calling this thing an experiment, because it's not going to work for everybody.

Obviously, it would have been disappointing for that lady, and no doubt many others. But with mediumship there are no guarantees. I can only try to access the spirit world, succeeding more often than not, but never succeeding every time.

Tony	Our next caller is Susan. Hello Susan.
James	Hello Susan.
Susan	Hello. I would just like to tell you that I felt something. I held my father-in-law's watch, which had stopped, and it suddenly set off.
James	When you're a channel for the other side, these things happen.

The psychic phenomena which were being reported by the people phoning in, were proving beyond any doubt, for me at least, that my psychic powers were indeed working. The look on Tony Newman's face, as caller after caller reported incredible experiences, somewhat amused me. The man looked totally and utterly astounded. My manager looked quite pleased with the results. He scribbled me one of his famous notes, it said 'you're a STAR my boy'. It did make me laugh.

Tony	Hello Julie, you're through to James.
Julie	Hello James.
James	Hello Julie.
Julie	I just wanted to say to you that I have seen a medium before, and tonight I actually went to bed early so I could listen to the programme. I held a photo of my father and looked at your name, and the experience I got is the experience I had with the medium, the whole of my body shakes. Anything other than that, I cry a lot when it happens, but it's as if the whole of my body has no control, it shakes and shakes.
James	It's very important this, could I just ask you what it is that upsets you? Is it because you miss your father, or is it because of something in the experience you have? What is it that upsets you?
Julie	Yes, I do miss him a lot. I miss him a lot, but I feel his presence in my house all the time.

James You see, this is the reality, these people are not dead, that's the truth of the situation. I mean, I'm sat here in this studio, with people ringing in from all over the place, saying who knows what's happening. I mean, that is proof.

I didn't know these people, they are surely not all gullible fools: to suggest that is an insult. This experiment did prove that my gift was real, beyond reasonable doubt at least.

Tony Our next caller is through to James.
Caller Hello, is that you James?
James Hello, love.
Caller Hello, lovey. I've longed for years and years to get through to my grandad, I was very, very close to him. I've had a medium here in my house and she's told me fantastic things, but never anything like this. I had his photograph in my hand, he was a gamekeeper and his face just split, I'm not a crank, his face seemed to go '3-D', that's the only thing I can say. I didn't get any feeling, nothing, but his face just seemed to go '3-D'.
James This was during the experiment, was it?
Caller Yes.
James Well, that's brilliant.

The calls continued through the night to 1am. I was absolutely exhausted, but exhilarated and delighted that we had proven a point.

Driving home with John, I pondered on exactly what we had just done. 'Did you listen to the reaction, it was incredible', I was enthusing to my manager. 'Wait till you do that on national TV, it will cause a sensation', he said. 'They'll never let me do that on the TV' I said, but at the back of my mind a little voice was saying 'Oh yes they will, and sooner than you think'. John just laughed and put a tape on the cassette player, 'let's listen to PJ Proby', he said, inflicting his former singing star on my weary ears. 'If he'd done what I told him, he'd be back at the top now.' The deep tenor voice of the legendary sixties superstar echoed round the car, he was singing the song John wrote for his failed comeback, 'Stage of Fools'. 'We can't all be winners, we can't always win . . .' I tried to join in. 'Stick to being a psychic, you sing like a horse', John said, full of praise and encouragement, as usual!

The Supernatural Experiment proved to be an amazing success. Both John Myers and Tony Newman were extremely pleased with the response, and said the telephone lines were jammed for many hours after I had left the station. Establishing the fact that for many thousands of listeners, my radio demonstration had opened the door, however briefly, to the world beyond.

The results of my psychic projection had certainly proven the veracity of my powerful gift, even if not to everyone. I am certain that Tony Newman understood, perhaps for the first time, that I was exactly what I claimed to be, a powerful channel for the other side.

John Myers had no doubts, he told his listeners the next morning how the long-broken lighter he held during the experiment had burst into flames. 'How he does it, I just don't know', he said, bemused by the whole supernatural experience.

The next day, my manager phoned me with some disquieting news. 'Radio Aire have contacted me, they want you on *The James Whale Show* next week'. Mr Whale had a reputation as a savage interviewer. I expressed my doubts to John about this. 'Don't worry, you'll sort him out', he said. Perhaps that was easier said than done, James Whale ate incompetents alive!

10

A Media Success

The night of 8 December 1991 was cool with just a hint of
Lancashire mist drifting in from the distant hills. I stood
outside my home in Bolton, patiently awaiting the arrival of my
manager, John, in his car. We were off for a potentially fiery
interview with probably the most notorious of presenters in the
British media, James Whale.

Radio Aire is situated in Leeds, Yorkshire. As we drove out
of Bolton, John and I discussed the strategy for dealing with
this often aggressive, and occasionally insulting man. 'James
tonight, you will put Mr Whale right. By the time you've
finished this programme, he will accept that your gift is the
genuine article'. John was once again building my confidence,
for an encounter with an unknown quantity. For all that I knew
about James Whale had been gleaned by observing him on his
network television programme, *The James Whale Radio Show*,
broadcast at 1am on network ITV. From those brief
observations I had formed the opinion that 'The Whale' was
quite capable of annihilating anyone who floundered in front
of his extremely acerbic and sometimes eccentric approach. I
had seen many big name stars disintegrate before his razorsharp
style. This man was the media's answer to Rocky Marciano.

However, the fact that my manager would be with me in the
studio gave me some form of confidence. I knew that John
would accept no messing about, and I gained some strength
from this knowledge. As it turned out, Mr Whale was far from

being the 'ogre' he had been painted. My friends all said he would terminate my career. In fact, the evening proved to be both enjoyable and informative.

In my experience, most presenters generally meet the guests they are going to interview, prior to going live on air. However, in the case of James Whale, this was not so. He insisted that we did not even see each other prior to the interview, was reluctant to permit my manager to enter the studio, and the producer took some time to persuade him to allow this to take place.

As we entered the studio, James Whale came up and shook our hands. He is a large man of burly build, but instead of the frown I so often see him wearing on television, he was, on this occasion, wearing a smile. The greeting was warm and friendly, and as we sat down he asked me how we would like to format that evening's show. This greeting was hardly the behaviour of an antagonistic aggressor, it put me immediately at my ease.

After a brief discussion, the three of us agreed that we would utilise 'The Psychic Experiment', as previously broadcast on Red Rose Gold Radio, and attempt to give the listeners of Radio Aire an experience of supernatural phenomena. James Whale would advise them, whilst I took the calls in which the events of the evening would be explained by myself.

As we prepared for the repeat of The Psychic Experiment, Linda, the programme producer, came into the studio and told James Whale that Radio Aire were receiving a number of telephone calls from unidentified callers, who were simply saying, 'this is very frightening', and then hanging up. James Whale calmly turned to Linda and said, 'I'm very pleased about that, I would be annoyed if they didn't'. This was indeed most encouraging and both John and myself were pleased to be in the presence of a man so obviously in control of the situation.

James advised the listeners to Radio Aire that evening that they were about to take part in an experiment, which could perhaps provide them with images from the next world.

He kindly permitted me to explain the extent and limitations of The Psychic Experiment which we were about to undertake.

He did, however, seem somewhat concerned that this may be a frightening experience, as opposed to a pleasant one. I was able to alleviate his worries and explain that this was far from being the case, indeed many would be comforted by the experience.

James took me to task about my reasons for requesting the presence of my manager in the studio. He suggested that this conveyed the impression that I was nothing more than a theatrical entertainer, a charge, as I have previously stated, that I am frequently presented with. He questioned John about how we came to be working together, and I intervened, explaining that the message I received from the spirit world when I saw John on the television directed me to find him and request that the man manage me. This had also been confirmed recently, when attending a spiritualist church in Lancashire. The medium taking the service gave me a message concerning John Sutton. The gist of the message being that I was about to become incredibly successful and that this success would be the direct responsibility of a man whose name was John. Her actual words were, 'The doors are about to open for you, James Byrne, and the man who will open all the doors is called John. You have just met this man John, and he is going to lead you right to the very top'.

I am not certain that James Whale and the listeners accepted this explanation as being the truth. It is, however, exactly that. I realise that it may seem an extremely unlikely explanation, but to someone who is psychic this is exactly the kind of experience which does take place. I hear voices, those voices tell me the truth, as simple as that.

I can spot a 'phoney' at the end of the street, it is absolutely impossible for people to lie through their teeth to me and expect me to believe them. It's as if a light shines above their head each time they try and tell me an untruth. With John Sutton, I got the impression that not only was he telling me the truth, but he was driving me on to success, where in the past I had simply experienced nothing but failure. His constant barrage of words, all directing me to succeed, altered my self perception.

I believed in him, and began to believe in myself.

James Whale explained to the listeners exactly how the supernatural journey would be undertaken. He advised his audience to write down my name and get a memento or photograph of someone who had passed on into the next world. The scene was set for Psychic Experiment Two.

I looked across at John who, by this time, was pouring coffee from the mauve flask and handing me a biscuit. The man seemed totally unperturbed, unlike myself – I was once again perspiring profusely. Though this experiment had worked exceptionally well at Red Rose Gold Radio, I was still uncertain as to the outcome of any future attempt, this one included. Perhaps it may be that I have less confidence than my manager, that didn't seem to matter to him, we were doing it anyway.

James Whale gave me a hard stare and announced to the public that this evening's experiment was being listened to by the producers of his network television show. 'Who knows, Mr Byrne, perhaps my producer can get you on television'. The mere thought of trying this in front of millions of people nationwide sent a tremor of trepidation down my spine. John's face lit up in delight, as if to say, that is exactly what we want.

James Whale introduced The Psychic Experiment: 'Ladies and gentlemen, tonight I want you to write down the name James Byrne on the top of a piece of paper. During the next minute, whilst James Byrne transmits his psychic powers, I want you to concentrate carefully upon his name and look at the photograph or memento that you are holding of a loved one who has departed. We are about to see whether or not, there is anything at all in this. STAND BY'.

He indicated to his desk controller and they began playing the music. 'Mars', from The Planets suite by Gustav Holst, was the selected piece. This extremely dramatic sound certainly would set the scene for the people listening to the radio show. I concentrated my psychic powers and, whispering a prayer to my spirit guides, asked them to permit the power to be set free.

As the music drew to a dramatic close, James Whale introduced the first caller.

Elsie   Hello James, I want to tell you I've just seen my
              father. I've just seen my dad, he was smiling at me.

James   How did that make you feel, my dear? Did it make
              you feel happy?

Elsie   Yes, it did. You see, he died thirteen years ago. I
              went to see him in hospital, but all that was there
              was the empty bed, he'd passed away.

James   You may be upset at this point, but I am sure it
              makes you feel happy to know that your father is
              there, and he is watching over you with love.

Elsie   Yes, that's right James.

The next caller reported that he had been holding a photograph
of his late grandmother. During The Psychic Experiment he
had seen this photograph come to life and heard the dear lady
who he had loved all his life speak to him from the spirit world.
I advised him that his grandmother was obviously intent on
expressing her love and affection for her grandson, who
remained in this material world.

At the end of this conversation, James Whale indicated his
utter disbelief in this last call. It seemed that Mr Whale was
unconvinced by the caller's account of his mysterious and
supernatural experience which he recounted on air. I personally
believed the man to be telling the truth and defended his report.
Obviously, it must take some nerve to ring into a radio station
and tell a cynical and experienced interviewer, such as James
Whale, that you have experienced a psychic phenomenon. One
is leaving oneself wide open to ridicule.

I realised that this may be somewhat off-putting to the
audience now tuned in to Radio Aire, but hoped that they
would respond positively if they had indeed witnessed the kind
of supernatural phenomena which were being reported. I had
every confidence that The Psychic Experiment had, once again,
been a success. John leant across and placed his hand heavily
upon my shoulder; 'you want some more coffee, superstar?' he
said, which cheered me no end. At least I knew that one person
in the studio was firmly on my side.

The calls continued to pour in. People reported various sorts of phenomena, varying from mere tingles down the spine to actual apparitions appearing before them. It certainly baffled and astounded 'The Whale'.

The entire demonstration that evening proved to be an exceptional success, and my initial worries absolutely unfounded. James Whale, whilst proving to be an adversary in certain respects, had generally been a very nice and considerate man. Totally unlike the obnoxious ogre I had imagined him to be.

It was a still, misty Yorkshire night as we drove silently over the hills out of Leeds, down the M62, heading back to Lancashire and my Bolton home. We talked quietly, going over the messages and the excitement of succeeding once again, with this incredible Psychic Experiment. John seemed extremely pleased that I was becoming an adept and articulate radio performer. For my own part, I considered the fact that I had survived in one piece without being savaged by the 'Rottweiler of the Radio Waves' to be success in its own right. 'Do that on national TV, James, and nobody can prevent you from attaining the goal we have collectively set out to achieve.' John's voice held conviction that night, it was a conviction that I was beginning to share, a belief that what we were doing would eventually lead us to demonstrate my gift before the biggest audiences in the entire world. It was almost as if we were being guided by a force beyond our understanding.

That night I had the strangest dream. I dreamt that John and I were standing at the top of a high staircase and in front of us was an open door. The dream really concerned me, I was extremely worried. When you start dreaming about your manager, it's time to find a girlfriend! If only there were more hours in a day, I thought, there is hardly time enough to fit in all the work that I feel it is necessary and my duty to do, let alone have time left to enjoy the company of a female friend. Perhaps the dream had been a premonition of achievements to come. We were certainly ascending the ladder of success. Nonetheless, I determined to contact one of my former girlfriends whom I had spoken to the previous week and suggest that we meet for an evening meal. Perhaps this would enable me to relax and take my mind off the forthcoming and extremely demanding period that was to be my life, under the exceptionally determined management of Mr Sutton. That man had changed my entire outlook. I could now conceive of myself as a person able to achieve success. It seemed that my spirit guides had been, as they always are, correct, in telling me to seek out my new manager.

Imagine my delight when the very next day, John Sutton telephoned my house to say that Mike Pearson of Yorkshire Television, the Executive Producer of the *James Whale Radio Show*, had invited me to appear on his programme on Friday 28th February 1992. 'I told you you were a star, my boy!', said John. I was beginning to believe him, but would always maintain my equilibrium. God gave me this gift, to enable others to share in my belief and understanding that there is life beyond the grave. He did not give it to me for use as a tool to promote JAMES BYRNE SUPERSTAR. The fact that I had a showbusiness manager did not mean that I, as a spiritualist, needed to be compromised. Obviously, I had to go along with John's presentation of my personal powers to a certain extent. It was, however, 'so far and no further': I was concerned that my gift be treated with due respect. He seemed determined that one way or another I would be the biggest thing in showbusiness. For my part, I was equally determined that my first duty was to my spiritual beliefs. It was, in the fullness of time, to produce some degree of disharmony between myself and the man to whom I had entrusted my career.

John Sutton was absolutely certain that the only way forward was for me to present myself as a dark and mysterious man. I believed that this was entirely the wrong direction for us to take. It caused a number of arguments, and in the end we agreed on a degree of compromise. This compromise seemed to work. It consisted of an external appearance which, in some ways, appeared sombre and mysteriously orientated but, when I opened my mouth to speak, the image shattered and I became the man that I really am, the boy from Bolton, James Byrne. A man of the people with a gift from God. Nothing will change that, neither fame, fortune, nor John Sutton will alter what I am.

My work in the Healing Clinic on Saturday mornings continued, despite the increased pressure from the theatrical presentations I was undertaking with John as my manager. One particular Saturday morning a lady whom I had known for many years came to see me with a problem that is peculiar to women only. She told me that the previous month she had discovered a lump in her left breast. Over the following weeks, this lump had grown to considerable proportions, and she was extremely concerned that it may be cancerous. Her visit to my clinic was to enable her to ask me for my psychic assessment of her medical complaint.

As I looked across at this middle-aged lady, eyes dark from the nights she had spent in a sleepless, troubled bed, I could sense that here was desperation personified. It touches my heart to see people who, at the very end of their tether, grasp at the remotest hope, whatever that may be. For so often, many people come to me in the belief that I am indeed their final chance. 'Please tell me, James, is it cancer?', she asked, tears brimming in her dark brown eyes. As I gazed deep, ever deeper into her, I could see that this was no cancer, this was in fact, a non-malignant growth, a cyst. I could hear a spirit voice say to me, as clearly as I hear anyone speak, 'This lady will survive'. I told her, 'go to your doctor, do not be afraid, what you have is a simple cyst. He will remove it and your sleepless nights, which are so evident, will return to peaceful slumbers'. Having visited me on many previous occasions with medical complaints of less complexity, this lady knew that I had spoken the truth.

Some days later, I was most pleased to learn from my mother that the woman in question had contacted her to say that my diagnosis had been correct. It was nothing more than the cyst I had told of, which the doctors had now removed. I was, once again, pleased to have been able to help a lady face up to what must, for some, be an exceptionally traumatic and trying time.

It may have been that without my assurance, that dear lady would have suffered in silence, in the sad and mistaken belief that her life was about to be terminated by that most feared of diseases, cancer.

My mother brought me a cup of tea that morning, and sensing my elation, asked if I had received further good news about my career. 'It's not about my career, mum, it's that lady who has been coming to see me for years, she's going to live.' It means so much to me, and I know my mother understands. She put her arms round me then and gave me a little hug, 'I'm right proud of you, Jim' she said, 'your tea's going cold'.

It's the wonderful, memorable moments like this that are the only proof I require. They confirm in myself the reason that God gave this gift to me, and that is why I will continue to work as a medium for as long as I live. The showbusiness paraphernalia and the elaborate stage presentations are all a mere front to enable me to extend my message and gift to the public. For without that, I would have no platform to present the powers which God has given to me. I personally believe that the media should, and must, be a part of my future. For without mass communication, I would be unable to present those powers to the majority of individuals throughout the world who are seeking proof of life after death. I truly believe that it is my destiny to do exactly that. People need to understand that there is a force beyond our earthly comprehension, that a next world exists, and it is for all of us, no matter what our colour or creed.

I continued to conduct services for the spiritualist churches in and around my area. Often I would be called away to places as far afield as Stockport or Blackpool, where I recently stood in for Doris Collins, who was taken ill at the time. For these demonstrations, no matter how far afield they may be, I take little or no expenses. Nor would I expect them. The only problems I find with limiting my demonstrations of psychic powers to spiritualist churches is that the general public are somehow afraid and rather reticent to attend such a church. The reasoning behind this is probably that spiritualism is, in many quarters, both frowned upon and taught against, especially by some of the established religions.

Whilst conducting a service at one Spiritualist Church, I gave a message to a gentleman called Norman. The message concerned his late wife who had recently passed over. After the service had ended, this gentleman came to me and said that during the message he had been extremely moved by my accuracy, and requested that I undertake a private reading for him in his own home. I agreed to do this, as I could see that Norman was extremely emotional about the loss of his wife.

When I visited him some weeks later, I was able to give very specific details concerning the life of his late wife, including her name. Norman, at the time, was a man in his late fifties. He seemed both alone and extremely distraught at the death of the one woman around whom his whole life had revolved. He told me that whilst she was alive, she had served the local Church of England cleaning and maintaining the flowers and general presentation of the premises. She had, he said, done many, many charitable works to raise funds for the church in which she had spent long and happy hours. The point he was trying to make to me was that since her death not one single member of her parish had been to console him and offer him help or guidance. Following the death of his dearly beloved wife he had felt abandoned. He told me that the only source of spiritual help he had received had been from my message at the Lytham Spiritualist Church. This seemed to me to be a sad indictment of people who profess to be caring and compassionate individuals. For I was, to this man, a complete and total stranger, albeit that I had the ability to communicate with his loved ones in the next world.

One incredible message I was able to give him concerned his sister in Liverpool. The spirit communicator told me that this lady was closely connected to two people called Thomas. The spirit said, 'It is Thomas the younger who will die'. I looked across at Norman and deep inside I knew that I had to tell this man the news, however saddening it might be. For the spirit had told me that Thomas the younger was a man of just 29 years. I felt that Norman would be able to offer his family the help and strength they required to proceed with their lives following the tragedy of this young man's premature demise. I knew that he would be able to support his sister in her time of sorrow, and therefore felt it my duty to explain exactly what the communicator had told me.

'The spirits tell me that Thomas the younger will die within a period of 12 months', I told Norman. He looked at me in utter incredulity. He had no doubt, however, that I had been speaking to the spirit of his late wife. The evidence she had given me was far too strong for there to be any shadow of doubt in that respect. Norman therefore accepted what I told him as the truth, and I am certain that this knowledge enabled him to offer his sister the strength and support she was undoubtedly going to require.

For the spirits never tell me lies. Some months later, Norman told me that his nephew, Tom, had died of cancer. 'Thank God you warned me, I hadn't seen my sister for ages and she needed my help', he said.

On 6 February 1992, I had been invited to attend Radio Merseyside to be interviewed by Linda McLoughlin. The interview began at 11am following the news, and I was expected to conduct The Psychic Experiment all over again. However, on this occasion I was not with my manager, John, I was all alone. It isn't so much that I mind being interviewed/ interrogated by people live on air, I do, however, expect to be treated with a modicum of respect. When managerial representation is absent on these occasions, it seems that some people think I am simply an entertainer seeking publicity and can be treated in any way that they see fit.

On this occasion, Linda McLoughlin decided to 'do a job' on me. Having suggested that I repeat The Psychic Experiment, she ran this into the news at 12 noon without any previous warning to myself. Despite the obvious distraction, I concentrated my powers and projected them to the best of my ability, right through the news broadcast. Linda McLoughlin was astounded when, following the news, the reports coming in from the listeners were exceptionally strong.

One lady contacted the station to say that during the demonstration of my psychic powers her wedding ring had appeared on the dressing-room table. This may not seem extraordinary, except for the fact that she had lost it, 24 years previously, when they lived in another part of the country. The ring had been apported from the spirit world.

Another lady contacted the station to say that her brother had been listening to Radio Merseyside whilst travelling along the A580 East Lancashire Road. As I was broadcasting my psychic powers, he heard the voice of his long dead father say to him, 'go and see your sister'. This caused a man in his middle years, a total disbeliever, to almost crash the vehicle he was driving. It did, however, have the effect that his late father desired, for the man turned off the motorway and drove towards his sister's house, where after 14 years of not speaking to each other following a minor family feud, they were reunited in tears of joy.

These and many other such reports flooded into Radio Merseyside as verification that, once again, despite being discomfited by a less than accommodating presenter, I had come up with the results.

It seems that wherever I go, people who are employed as interviewers on local radio stations take great delight in attempting to make me look something less than capable. Fortunately for me, the spirits are always there to help and guide me. As Edith Johnson Guy so often told me, 'trust in the spirits, James', and they never let me down.

That night, I went to see John in his home at Leyland. I was becoming increasingly concerned about my ability to cope with network television and the potentially aggressive James Whale. This was despite the fact that we had already met the gentleman on Radio Aire. It seemed to me that there was within this man a capability to attack and destroy. 'Don't worry', said John, 'I've spoken to Mike Pearson and I will be on the show with you. Mike tells me that there are a couple of vicars going on the show from the Church of England, one of whom is an official exorcist. I am sure that we are both looking forward to meeting these people'. John looked as if he really was, and

I could sense that he was relishing any confrontation which may take place. On the other hand, I was personally terrified. These people belonged to the recognised and accepted established religion of the United Kingdom, whilst I was a member of the Spiritualist Church, announcing to the world that I was able to communicate with the spirits. A practice which I understood the Church would condemn.

I asked John what the format was for the presentation on network television. 'We're going to do The Psychic Experiment, and blow the mind of the United Kingdom', he said. Once again, I saw the mad glint in my manager's eyes, only this time it did not make me doubt his sanity, I knew it meant determination. Mary, his wife, brought us a cup of coffee. 'Is he going on at you again?' she said. 'You want to watch him Jim, I think he's nuts at times.'

Considering what John had got me lined up for, I thought Mary had a point. 'Be all right' he laughed, 'only a few million people watching us.' I'm sure he enjoyed winding me up, but perhaps that is exactly what I needed to succeed. In that respect, only time would tell. In the meantime, my hands trembled uncontrollably every time I considered what might happen.

11

Trial By Television

My new manager had signed me to demonstrate at Leeds City Varieties Theatre in Yorkshire. This was a venue at which I had appeared on a number of occasions in the past. I had always done good business, but this time John insisted that we would sell it out. How we were going to do that was 'his baby', not mine. Nonetheless, he seemed very certain that we would succeed.

To enable us to do this, he contacted a number of local radio stations, including BBC Radio Leeds, who invited me to attend for interview on 8 February 1992. John and I set off on a pleasant afternoon and drove into the centre of Leeds, looking forward to a reasonable verbal exchange of ideas during a nice informal interview with one of the BBC's most experienced presenters, Mr Peter Levy. This interview was part of a wider campaign set up by John to promote our forthcoming presentation at the world famous City Varieties Theatre. Many people will recognise this venue as being the site of *The Good Old Days*, a popular network TV series in which members of the audience, dressed in Edwardian costume, were filmed watching vaudeville acts performed by stars of today.

We arrived at BBC Leeds, some thirty minutes prior to our forthcoming interview on air. As usual, they were extremely hospitable and brought us hot black coffees to drink in the waiting room. John assured me that this would prove to be an exceptional success. 'You're going to startle them', he said. It seemed to me at that time that there was nothing I could not do, according to John Sutton. I sincerely hoped that he was right.

We were led into the studio by a young female production assistant. She introduced us to the presenter, Peter Levy, who invited me to sit down and face the microphone. At these times, I am always aware that my abilities are being tested. It is a form of public scrutiny, an examination of the veracity of my psychic powers.

Peter's initial questioning of me indicated that he thought I was little more than a con artist, and he made no effort to disguise his disbelief. This is an allegation which I am frequently required to rebut. It implies that the public, who pay good money to see me, are extremely gullible, and that, in my experience, is just not the truth. The public will only accept verifiable evidence, that means the information I am giving must be correct. By correct, I mean exact to the point where it cannot be a good guess. For instance, it would be extremely unlikely for me to be able to guess the christian name and surname of an individual's parents. Nor would it be likely that I could guess the address at which this person had lived whilst alive. This is the kind of information I pass, to establish the identity of the spirit attempting to communicate through me.

Yet tricksters and magicians, such as Paul Daniels, claim that this is nothing but an elaborate sham. Mr Daniels has quite recently extended his remit to insulting Jesus Christ, so what chance would I have of convincing such a hardened sceptic. In my opinion, he should be very careful what he says about matters of which he obviously knows nothing, because like us all, in the fullness of time, Paul Daniels will be required to account for his actions, and I know he's in for a big surprise. The question is, will he like it – I suspect the answer to be 'not a lot'.

Audiences at my presentations are often only too eager to pick holes in the information and messages that I give. Generally speaking, ninety per cent of these people, will never have witnessed the presentation of a medium before. They come to assess and question, if necessary, the messages and information which are passed. I would not have this any other way, because if everyone were willing to accept any old rubbish, the world would be full of charlatans and frauds passing themselves off as psychics. There are very few who can replicate the accuracy of my information, which is given to me from the spirit world – by accuracy, I mean actual names and addresses, not just generalisations.

Peter Levy suggested that we test my powers by accepting the first call and getting me to read for that person, live on air. I accepted the challenge, explaining that whilst I could make no specific demands upon my gift, I would do my absolute utmost to ensure that what I gave was verifiable evidence.

Mr Levy suggested to me that it would be better if somebody who was a believer phoned in, unlike himself, a total non-believer. I explained that the only problem I might face was being confronted live on air with an absolute bigot. Such people deny truth and I would be unable to pass a message to them. My experience is that when you give evidence to bigots, they refute it. All I requested was that the caller have an open mind, and given such a situation, I felt certain I would be able to respond positively.

Peter introduced Jessie, the lady who had managed to get through to BBC Leeds. I spoke to this young woman as calmly as I could, given the fact that I was under quite a considerable amount of stress in that difficult situation.

Peter	Jessie, good morning.
Jessie	Good morning.
Peter	What would you like James to try and do?
Jessie	Well, if he could bring me one of my family, you know.
James	Yes, but don't tell me anything about who they are, or anything.
Jessie	No.
James	Well, before we start this, have I met you before?
Jessie	No, I have never seen you love, in my life.

James   Well, can I just ask you a question love, and the
           BBC forgive me for this. Have the BBC set me
           up, tell me the truth, have they asked you to do
           this?

Jessie   No, I have just rung in on the spur of the
           moment.

James   As long as I know that love, I am prepared to co-
           operate all the way. I'll tell you one thing I want
           to say to you, now you must bear in mind that
           these things take more than a minute to do, so
           bear with me on that. Now don't tell me
           anything, all I want you to do is listen to what I
           say to you. If you agree with it, say yes, if you
           don't, say no. Is that fair?

Jessie   Yes.

James   Now, as soon as you started to speak a man's name
           came into my mind, but I'm not going to tell you
           that name for a minute, I'm going to tell you
           something about this man first. Whoever he was,
           before he died he had a terrible problem with his
           breathing, or his chest. It was definitely in the
           chest area. Now then, he also makes me aware of
           three children. Are you one of three children, or
           have you got three children?

Jessie   Yes. Well, I am one of four actually.

James   No, no, I didn't say four, darling.

Jessie   But, I can understand that part.

James   I'll talk more about that later, because something
           about three children seems significant with you.

Jessie   It is, it is love, I'll tell you . . .

James   No, no, Jessie you must not tell me, let me tell
           you, we'll come to that in a minute. But the thing
           I want to get across to you about this, is when I
           look at your family, it's as though there's been
           two marriages or two families that have sort of
           rolled into one.

Jessie   That's true, that's why there's four of us.

James   I see what you mean.

Jessie   That's why I can understand it.

James   But let me stress love, that the three children I believe have the same parents. Maybe the fourth one didn't belong to the three, I don't know. But I do believe that the three children, one of which is you, belong to the same mum and dad. Now, the thing that struck me about this, of your two parents, your mother stands out to me much more than your dad does. So, I am inclined to think that she was the one who was either married twice, or somehow came by these step-relations. Is that true?

Jessie   Yes, that's true.

James   Also, I know it's a very common name, but the name of William stands out a mile with you.

Jessie   That's my husband.

James   That's your husband. I know a lot of people are going to say, 'Well, I've got a husband called William', but who cares as long as it's right, nobody can argue.

Jessie   Well, that's my son as well, he's called William.

James   Now then love, also isn't it true, that somebody, somebody very close to you, is going to pick up a new car very soon, or have they just done that?

Jessie   My son has. Well, it's not brand new, it's secondhand, but he's just got another one.

James   Yes, but it's only just happened.

Jessie   Yes.

James   Now then, is that car red?

Jessie   Yes.

James   I thought it was, because I am aware of all this you see. I am very much aware of the name William. Now, I'll be honest with you, I know that you said he was your husband, I don't know whether that man's died or not, but I do have a sad feeling that seems to attach itself to that name.

Jessie	Well, we were divorced.
James	You don't have to go into personal details.
Jessie	No, but what I mean is, that's why you got the sad feeling.
James	Yes, well that might be the reason love, it's just that I have a sad feeling about that particular name. But you see, if you remember, at the beginning of this I mentioned to you that I was aware of a man who's suffered tremendously with his chest or breathing, it was either his chest or his heart, because it was in his chest.
Jessie	It was my father.
James	Now this man's name was John. Now then, so that might not be your father.
Jessie	No, it isn't love. My son's called John.
James	No, but your son's still living love. This man I am aware of called John, he says that most people called him Jack, he says I have to mention the shop.
Jessie	Oh, my grandad!
James	Well, what was the shop, tell me what the shop was?
Jessie	Well, I've had a few shops lately, so I don't know which one it is.
James	Well, as long as you've had one, that's all I'm bothered about. But he says, I have to mention that you see. But the thing is, he told me all this about your son, he mentioned William, and you know, I don't know whether I should say this or not, I am not just saying this to be nice to you, but he says, it was all William's fault.
Jessie	Yes, that's true.
James	I can sense in that tone that you want me to shut up now, but anyway that's basically it. Now, apart from having this son, William, don't you have a daughter as well?
Jessie	Yes.

James   Isn't she your only daughter?

Jessie   Yes.

James   I thought so, because she's the only one I'm aware of. Now then, the three children are obviously the three that your mum had, one of which is you. So, just tell me, I know that you said there's been four, but just confirm for me, wasn't that fourth one either a half-sister or brother, or step-sister or brother?

Jessie   Well, I've got a half-brother and a half-sister as well.

Peter   Good grief!

James   That's right. Well, we'll leave it at that darling. (I could see the presenter reeling back in his chair, shocked and amazed at my very accurate reading. Proof indeed.)

Peter   Jessie, thank you very much indeed, we're grateful to you. Well, I have to say, that is unbelievable and as a disbeliever, it's even more unbelievable.

I personally think that Peter Levy was rather astounded by what I had just done. It certainly seemed to impress the listeners, who bought every single ticket available for my presentation at the City Varieties on 20 February 1992. There is no feeling quite like presenting before a full house, I was really looking forward to the night. John was again proved right!

That evening at Leeds City Varieties, I was undertaking the presentation using a new format designed by my manager. John had insisted that we try a change of image. Throughout my career to date, I had always presented my psychic powers in a straightforward and down-to-earth manner. As this subject is so controversial, I felt that the inclusion of a theatrical presentation would reduce the credibility of my gift. Mr Sutton decided that we would do it his way! So, on the night of 20 February 1992 for the first time in my entire career, I agreed to be presented in a manner which, to some extent, went against my personal spiritualist beliefs.

The entire auditorium was plunged into darkness, and at the instructions of my manager, I sat centre stage with a table and two candles burning in brass candlesticks, making the whole effect extremely eerie. I could hear the audience gasp as the curtains drew back, revealing James Byrne, myself, dressed entirely in black – black suit, black shirt, totally black. I felt a right pudding! I knew what to do next, I sent the whole thing up! For this is not how spiritualists or mediums operate, seated in the dark with candles burning, and people clutching hands expecting the table to lift, or hear rapping noises from the spirit world to startle and astonish those observing the proceedings. The spirits who would be observing this must have been enjoying a very good laugh. In no time at all, the audience and myself were joining them.

Though it had been John's idea to create a rather spooky atmosphere for the first thirty seconds, we agreed that this was to be little more than a spoof, to enable me to capture the attention of my audience, ninety per cent of whom would never have witnessed the demonstration of a genuine medium on any previous occasion. It worked brilliantly.

When I came off after the first half, John slapped me firmly on the back, as he always does on such occasions, nearly fracturing my spine, and told me that this was, to date, my most effective presentation. That, I must admit, is exactly how I felt. The audience responded magnificently and the whole evening was an exceptional success.

On that night, I gave one particular message which sticks clearly in my mind. I was receiving information from a spirit who told me his name. 'My name is Jeff', he said, 'I fell and killed myself, it was an accident.' A lady in the audience accepted this information, saying that Jeff was one of her relatives. The spirit gave me far more detailed information concerning his demise, which I was unable to pass in public, for Jeff had been killed whilst burgling a house. I could not pass this information in front of 600 people, it would have embarrassed the lady recipient a great deal. I can remember that she said to me, 'I don't wish to talk about this anymore'. I respected her feelings and terminated the message, despite the fact that the spirit was anxious to communicate with her.

I was really enjoying this presentation at the City Varieties Theatre and the audience was receiving my messages extremely well. Then, for some reason I cannot explain, a spirit came showing me hats, attempting to get a message across to me without words, but showing me a vision of hats or helmets. He showed me a policeman's helmet, a fireman's helmet. This was part of a message that he was attempting to give to me, so I gave this information out to the audience. I could hear him whisper a name which I spoke aloud and told the audience that I was receiving images of hats or helmets. It took me quite some considerable time to find the person for whom this message was intended. The audience was in uproar, when the lady said 'that man lived in an area of Leeds called Elmett'. Quite amazing!

The spirits will use whatever methods they can to communicate through me. Obviously, this particular spirit had selected the vision he gave me as part of his method of passing the information he wanted his loved one to receive. It caused the audience to laugh a great deal. Nonetheless, the message was correct and that is what concerns me most of all.

I enjoyed that evening in Leeds very much indeed. It is an exceptionally warm venue and one in which I have always been made most welcome. Due, no doubt, to the most positive management of Peter Sandeman, who gives his public exactly what they want, quality entertainment at the right price.

The pleasures of presenting at City Varieties were soon almost forgotten. I had something else to worry about now, the forthcoming demonstration on the *James Whale Radio Show* for network ITV. The whole idea somewhat terrified me. John seemed less than anxious about my abilities and, as he always did, assured me that I would be a success. The problem was, if I failed in this trial by television, the whole of the country would be watching and marking me down as a failure. It was something I simply could not afford to be at this stage in my career. We had been working very conscientiously towards achieving national recognition. Public humiliation at this point would result in returning to home base and having to start all over again. My credibility as a public presenter of psychic powers would be nil, and it was for this reason that I was concerned. How we could ensure that we gained a success neither myself, nor John Sutton knew, we simply had to trust in the spirits.

A lot of my acquaintances had requested tickets to attend the *James Whale Radio Show* at Yorkshire Television, and the presenters of the programme forwarded me a number of complimentaries, to enable my friends and family to gain entrance. I passed these out and all were exceptionally pleased that they were going to see me presenting on national television. John had also received some tickets and sent these out to members of the press who he knew, including Cliff Bell of the *Lancashire Evening Post*, who had covered some stories about my career to date.

During the week leading up to the show I became more and more nervous. At night, I would phone John for his opinions as to what he thought would happen. He seemed less than his usual positive self. This made me even more nervous. The problem was that neither of us knew exactly what we would be faced with when the cameras started to run and we were live on network television.

When we arrived at Yorkshire Television's studios in Leeds, we were greeted by Mike Pearson, the producer of the *James Whale Radio Show*. Mike, who was wearing a shirt which looked like the interior of Kew Gardens, explained that they were not going to permit members of my family or my friends to sit in the studio audience. He seemed to think that we would attempt to set the audience up, to receive and respond to any messages which I may give. This did, to a certain extent, perturb me. I knew that people had travelled a long way across the country to be in the studio to watch their friend being filmed on network television, and there was absolutely nothing I could do about it. We were entirely in the hands of Yorkshire

Television and they had decided that only people they had issued complimentary tickets to would be permitted into the studio for the show.

We were taken to the makeup department, to receive a light dusting of powder to take away any shine which might reflect in the bright lights of the television studio. Whilst John and I were having this done, James Whale told us that during the evening, preparations for the show had gone dramatically wrong. 'Everything's been happening here', he said, 'the whole thing has been a real mess today.' James Whale looked surprisingly concerned, he did not seem his usual ebullient and confident self. I am certain it had nothing to do with me, but perhaps my spirit guides were intervening on my behalf.

With less than fifteen minutes to go to live presentation, I was becoming increasingly nervous. Both John and I were very angry that people that we had issued complimentary tickets to were being excluded from the studio. We didn't want to set the audience up, all we wanted to do was to ensure that the people who had travelled all this way got what they had come to see – after all they did have tickets.

Finally prepared for the show, dressed in my stage clothes, totally black, John and I proceeded to the studio and took our seats opposite James Whale. He had prepared a rudimentary set, which consisted of an open table with three candles burning in a silver candelabra. The credits ran and we were live on network TV.

James Whale Good evening and welcome to a live show from Leeds tonight. You can probably sense that its just slightly different. Tonight, we are going to embark on a little bit of television history. We are going to try a television experiment that has never been done before, an experiment in psychic matters. All during rehearsals, funny things have gone wrong, we've had problems, but we hope to find out answers to questions people have been asking for years. Good evening, James.

James Byrne Good evening James.

James Whale That's going to be very confusing as well! I would like to introduce John, who is James's manager and agent. Before we go any further, James is what, a psychic, or what would you describe him as, a medium?

John Well, I would describe him as a psychic, he is definitely a medium, there is no doubt about that. He is a medium for the next world, the spirits use James Byrne as a channel to communicate with this world.

James Whale He's sort of a male version of the late Doris Stokes.

John Yes, except that he does not wear a pink dress!

Can't take that manager of mine anywhere!

James Whale asked me to describe how I would undertake the United Kingdom's first network TV Psychic Experiment. I outlined the requirements, the usual photograph or memento and writing down my name, James Byrne, concentrating on this whilst I projected the powers over the television airwaves. James Whale himself looked extremely concerned. For my own part, I was equally terrified. Would this work? It amounted to a public examination of my gift, a form of trial.

Following a brief interlude in which the two vicars were interviewed by James Whale, I was led back into the studio and seated before the cameras and invited to project my powers, taking the United Kingdom on a journey into the unknown. Mike Pearson had arranged some really weird music and, as this began to play, I concentrated all my psychic force and asked the spirits to free the power. This is what happened next.

James Whale Okay, here is a call now. Mandy hello.
Mandy Hello.
James Whale Mandy, where are you calling from?
Mandy From Birmingham.
James Whale Has anything happened to you Mandy?

Mandy   Yes, it did. I saw what I thought was a black box
               and a figure. It was the figure of my grandmother.
               I am shaking like a leaf here. She was holding a
               musical box, which she gave me just before she
               died. I was about 6 then, I'm now 23. I don't
               remember gran very well, but I remember the
               musical box very clearly, and that was all I could
               see. Quite honestly, it's frightened the life out of
               me. I'm shaking.

James Whale Have you ever seen anything like that before
               Mandy?

Mandy   No way, never.

James Whale Did it in any way try to harm you, or did you
               think it was going to do anything nasty?

Mandy   No. It was my gran and it was a very special
               musical box that was very precious to her. I don't
               know what that man did, but he's marvellous, he
               really is.

James Byrne I am pleased that you've said that. It is wonderful
               that someone I have never met has rung in, saying
               what has happened to them. I do not think this
               girl is shaking because any harm was done to her,
               it's the shock, it startles people, because it's
               there, it's real, it's proof.

Following the initial call and the first response to The Psychic
Experiment, James Whale asked me to demonstrate my psychic
readings to the studio audience. This is always extremely
difficult to do on television, because of the very pressured
situation that people are in. I have seen numerous mediums
fail, whom I know to be extremely gifted and genuine, notably
on the James Randi Show.

However, on this occasion I decided to try, attempting to give
correct readings to the audience. This proved to be somewhat
less than totally convincing, and it was not until the show had
finished that I discovered that the actual message was intended
for the wife of one of the vicars, who was with me being

interviewed at the time. It also struck me as being very strange that whilst one lady could receive one of the messages I had given, her relations who were sat at the other side of the studio, could not accept the same information when I spoke to them. This often happens, either they forget or are too overawed by the situation to respond correctly. When this happens, it makes me look less than effective.

In the future, I intend to avoid such situations in all television demonstrations, it does nothing at all for my credibility.

James Whale then requested that the callers be put through and this is the response that we received.

Nicole   My boyfriend died in a car crash and he gave me a ring before he died. I was sitting watching James Byrne and concentrating, when I felt a presence behind me and heard a whisper, it was my boyfriend's voice, saying my name closely near my ear. As I looked around, the curtains were moving and I could hear some singing in the distance.

James Whale What sort of singing?

Nicole   It was a song that we used to like, when we first met in a bar, it was the song that was playing, he was singing the melody to it.

James Whale Okay Nicole, thank you very much indeed.

One of the vicars, who was sitting opposite me, intervened at this point, explaining that this was possibly little more than imagination working overtime for the girl in question, who had heard her dead boyfriend singing the song that had been playing when they had first met. Some people will just not accept the truth.

Following a degree of verbal interaction between myself and Olwyn, the vicar, James Whale introduced the next caller.

James Whale Hello Liz.

Liz   Hello. I was watching James Byrne and was very sceptical, I didn't think anything would happen, my mother died November last year and I was sitting holding her purse. I have two clocks in my living room, both of them were reading the same time, midnight. When I looked at the clocks after James had been on the television, 5 minutes later approximately, one clock was 5 minutes further on than the other. The strange thing is, that whilst I have been waiting to come on the line to you, both of the clocks show the same time now.

James Whale You're not pulling my leg are you?

Liz I am *not* pulling your leg, my daughter is here. I am baffled and absolutely flabbergasted.

James Whale For me, I wonder why on earth the spirits are doing these little things. Obviously James, are you saying it's just to show they are there?

James Byrne Communication is very difficult and I think spirit people will communicate in any way possible for them to do so, it is not always in the most obvious way, in the form of a voice or vision.

Tom, the clergyman-exorcist, intimated that my role in this was purely one of autosuggestion. I have already expressed my feelings on this, it is simply not the case. People ring in and tell me that these psychic experiences have taken place. I do not implant in their minds, the nature of any supernatural phenomenon that may occur.

I could sense that James Whale was extremely agitated by the nature of the phone-calls that were being received. These, to me at least, were absolute proof of the veracity of my psychic powers. It surely cannot be the case, that on any given night, thousands and thousands of people throughout the United Kingdom are all experiencing the kind of psychic phenomena which were being reported on the show. If this was the case, there would be a national inquiry into the nature of it. These phenomena only take place in such frequency during my psychic projections, and the reports proved beyond reasonable doubt that I had this incredible ability.

The next positive call came from a man in Lincolnshire.

James Whale Hello Rob.

Rob   Hello there. I would just like to say that I have never believed in anything to do with the supernatural before in my life 'til now. My grandpa died 12 years ago, he had brought me up from a child as my father had left when I was two years old. The only thing he ever left me was a statue of a racehorse called Najinski, which is sitting by my television screen. I was just sitting there and this name came on the TV, James Byrne. He said concentrate on his name, so I concentrated and the whole room went totally cold. Whether this was a sign, I just don't know.

James Whale You said before that you did not believe in this sort of mumbo jumbo, has this experience left you in two minds now?

Rob   That's right, definitely. The whole room went totally cold even though the central heating was on. It was really, really cold. You know the saying, 'when people walk over your grave, the hairs stand up on the back of your neck', it was just like that.

This gentleman from Lincolnshire was reporting the kind of phenomenon which I would expect to be related to a visit from the next world. Once again, evidence that my powers were projecting extremely well. I was very pleased that people were able to receive proof of the existence of life beyond the grave.

James Whale From Manchester, our final call, Ian. Hello.

Ian   Hello. My father died about two years ago, he was ill for ten years with a bad chest. He used to believe that gargling and swallowing TCP would make it a bit better. I was holding his cigarette case and concentrating on the name, when I got this very strong smell of TCP. I don't use TCP, we haven't any in the house.

Olwyn   (vicar) People have told me, we have got a ghost, we haven't seen the ghost, but when we go into the room where the ghost has been, there is a lovely fragrance.

Olwyn had confirmed that such experiences were within his knowledge. He seemed to me, a very nice and genuine man, who accepted that my gift was the real thing.

James Whale thanked us very much for attending and the show was over. The trial had ended. I believe that my powers had been proven.

Travelling home that evening with John, I felt totally and utterly drained of all my energy. We were both pleased with the way the show had turned out, even though it was less than enthusiastically received by the studio audience. This was due mainly to the pressurised situation. Cliff Bell of the *Lancashire Evening Post* told us that he had been almost unable to gain entrance, despite having a ticket, and being a member of the legitimate press.

On Monday morning, Mike Pearson from Yorkshire TV contacted my manager, to tell him that the station had been swamped with telephone calls recounting strange experiences following the first UK network TV Psychic Experiment.

One woman told Mike that whilst she was watching the transmission, a man had materialised at the side of her television set and said to her, 'Do not be afraid, I am your Guardian Angel'. Her boyfriend, who was sitting next to her at the time, had been so startled by this, that he had jumped up and run out of the house. Mike told me that he had not been seen since.

It seems they received in total over 5,000 telephone calls reporting various stages of supernatural phenomena. If this is not evidence of the veracity of my psychic powers, I do not know what is.

12

Haunted Houses

One of the questions I am frequently asked as a psychic is, why do we have such things as haunted houses?

The point is, everywhere in the whole world is haunted, if that is the term you select, it is just that most people cannot observe the spirits that occupy these places. It is my personal understanding that spirits do not in actual fact go anywhere, they exist in this world at a different form of vibration, and they are at times around us. Very often, the spirits will try and communicate their feelings of distress or anger to the people who are living in the material world which we exist in.

One such instance involving a spirit which was angered by the actions of living people concerned a lady in the town of Bolton where I live. Late one Sunday evening, it would be perhaps 11pm, I heard at my front door a loud banging. When I answered the door, there were two men present who requested that I attend their house.

'We are all frightened stiff, the house is definitely haunted, you've got to come and sort it out, James'. I looked at these two gentlemen, who were extremely distraught. It seemed that a presence had been occupying their home and causing them a great deal of consternation. They had absolutely no idea who this spirit was.

'It's the shape of an old lady, who keeps standing on our staircase', they told me. Dressing quickly in my large overcoat, I climbed into the car with them and they took me to their home, which was on a housing estate approximately three miles away from my home.

As soon as I went into the house, I became aware of the spirit of a lady who had passed very recently. I could hear her calling to me from up the staircase. As I went towards the top of the stairs, I saw standing before me the form of a woman who would perhaps be, whilst alive, in her late sixties or early seventies. She seemed extremely perturbed, and as I came close to her, she said, 'I am not leaving this house until I have spoken to my daughter'. I could clearly see this woman, she was dressed in ordinary outgoing clothes, with a little scarf at the back of her head. Her face looked extremely angry and she pointed down the stairs as if to indicate that I had to go and fetch her daughter for her.

When I told this to the people who had sent for me in the first place, the two gentlemen and the lady in the house, they looked extremely unhappy.

'It sounds like my grandmother', she said. 'Well', I told them, 'you had better go and fetch her daughter, because until she speaks to her, that spirit is going nowhere. In fact, she seems very determined'. On receiving this information, the two gentlemen jumped into their car and drove off to the other side of Bolton to collect the lady in question. I sat down and had a cup of tea, quite at ease with the whole affair, I had seen this so many times before.

Approximately three quarters of an hour later they returned, and in the car was the daughter of the spirit who was, at this point in time, occupying the top of the staircase.

'You'd better go up and have a word with this lady', I said, 'she's determined to speak to you, for some reason of which I am unaware. I'll come with you.' Together, we went up the stairs and as we reached the top, I saw again the shape of this little old woman in spirit form.

People do not believe that spirits look the same as human beings, but I can assure you that this lady looked as real as anybody else. In fact, she stood very close to her daughter, albeit that her daughter could not see her.

'Ask her why she didn't carry out my last wishes and bury me with my husband', the lady said in a tone of great anguish. 'Tell her, I am not pleased to have been cremated, I wanted to be buried. Ask her why she did it to me?'

I put this question to the spirit's daughter and observed that this information absolutely startled her. 'Well, it was cheaper to cremate her than bury her. We hadn't got a lot of money at the time'. That seemed to be the answer, but it did not please the spirit, who looked as if she was about to strike her daughter a severe blow to the side of the head. I looked across at the spirit and asked her if she was prepared to accept the explanation that her daughter had just given.

'Tell her, I'm not happy, but if that's the best she can do, well, that's it then', she said. Then she turned away and walked off to her appointed place.

When we went downstairs, I talked through this incident with the owners of the house and the spirit's daughter, explaining that often spirits do return when they are exasperated by the actions of people who remain in this world. It was, of course, beyond their power to rectify what they had already done, but the spirit, I felt, would never return, having now passed on that message of disgruntlement from the world beyond. I can assure you that the people in that house were absolutely startled by what I had told them, and they never reported any further instances of hauntings. The spirit had returned to her appointed place and left those in this material world to get on with their lives in peace.

One morning, my mother received a telephone call from a lady who requested that I attend her home, following a series of strange phenomena taking place. She told my mum that the electric lights would switch on of their own accord, doors would open and close, and in the house there was a feeling of very severe cold around one particular spot. She needed help.

I telephoned the lady in question and arranged to attend her premises, in an agreed effort to ascertain the nature of the problem. I must admit that it did sound to me like a typical case of a spirit attempting to communicate its disquietude.

Possibly unable to proceed, tied to our material world by some earthly memory, the spirit remained.

The residence in question was located at the end of a very long, desolate road. The moorland surrounding the house was extremely bleak and dreary. Trees bereft of leaves stood stark against that harsh landscape. The lady of the house invited me in and with a very worried look, offered me a cup of tea. I sat in a large, elaborately-furnished living room, littered with copies of *The Times*, *Horse and Hound*, *Tatler* and various other upmarket publications, listening to her accounts of the hauntings which were frightening her away from the premises.

I asked to be given a tour of the sites where psychic phenomena had been taking place. As we entered the basement area, I became aware that this was the centre of the problem.

'Please leave me alone here, I need to concentrate', I told the lady. She gave me a very strange stare, and returned to the living room above.

In the basement area, I sensed that about me there was a spirit, whose life had been ended by its own hand. As I concentrated and prayed, requesting that my spirit guide lead me in this enquiry, a man entered the room from the far end of the basement. I looked across and saw the shape of this man, in his mid-thirties, walk directly through the solid brick wall. In his hand he held a tombstone, and it was to this tombstone that he was pointing. As he approached me, I could see the desperation in his eyes, he pointed at the writing and in a deep male voice said, 'What's all this about then?' He walked to the centre of the basement area and pointed to the beams, which supported the floors above. 'I hung myself here', he said, and with that, picked up his tombstone and walked out through the opposite wall.

When I told the lady of the house what I had seen in the basement, she began to cry softly. 'That was my husband', she said, 'he hung himself in the cellar late last year and since that time, we have been experiencing very weird happenings in and around the building.' I told her that the man had showed me a large tombstone and said, 'What's all this about then?'

'Well, we have been having a great deal of problem agreeing on what to write on his tombstone. You see, because he killed himself, we are somewhat at a loss as to what to put', she said. I could sense that the lady was now able to accept that she must resolve this problem, for it seemed to be creating the anguish for her late husband.

'Can you tell him that we will resolve this, and ask him if he will leave us in peace', she said. I agreed to do this, assuming I could contact the spirit again, and returned to that cellar area for a second encounter with the restless spiritual form of her late husband.

As I stood in the basement, requesting and praying for help, the man walked through the wall once again. 'You know why I killed myself, I found her in bed with my daughter's boyfriend', the spirit told me. 'Tell her, I can never forgive her for that, but if she corrects the problems and leaves my daughter to live her life in peace, I will quit this awful house forever.' The spirit had spoken an unpalatable truth that I had to pass to his wife.

When I told the lady what her late husband had said, she began to weep profusely. 'How on earth could you know all this', she said, almost desperate that someone knew of her terrible secret. You see, people simply do not believe, despite the evidence I give, that what I tell them is the absolute and utter truth. No one but her husband, herself, and her daughter's boyfriend, knew that this affair had taken place. The knowledge had so devastated her husband that he had gone to the basement area and hung himself from the beams, so that now his spirit walked the house, determined to rectify the wrongs that were still taking place in the material world of which he was no longer a member.

Whether or not that lady did terminate her incestuous affair is beyond my knowledge. I only know that if she didn't, then the troubled spirit that was her husband will forever more walk the house where she lives, for his unquiet soul cannot proceed to its appointed place. Bound by the horror of his earthly experiences to seek redress, the spirit is trapped.

In the Lancashire town of Bamber Bridge, near Preston, there is a hotel called the Deans Court. In early October 1991, I received a telephone call requesting that I attend these premises to investigate a psychic phenomenon which was disrupting the running of the establishment. I agreed to investigate.

Myself and John Sutton attended the Deans Court Hotel, to make enquiries into the nature of these disturbances. Dean Hosker, the proprietor, told me that his chambermaids had been noticing a series of unusual happenings, the lights would switch on and off for no apparent reason, and in one instance the central electric candelabrum in a series of five had remained on, whilst the other four, for no explicable reason, had themselves switched off. The Electricity Board were unable to locate any fault in the system, throwing no light on this matter whatsoever.

A blue haze had been appearing in and around various points in the restaurant, particularly in one part which had recently been the subject of building alterations. In the basement area, staff were complaining of icy cold patches which instantly created themselves around them and, equally instantaneously, disappeared. There were reports of items being moved and, without explanation, found in other parts of the hotel. The general atmosphere was becoming extremely tense.

'I simply need somebody to put a stop to all this strange nonsense', said Dean. 'I've heard you on the radio, and read about you in the papers, and from what I am told, you can do the job'. I looked across at Dean, he certainly looked like a worried man.

'Well, I can only try', I said, and with that began my psychic search of the Deans Court Restaurant and Hotel.

I requested, as I always do, that this search be conducted by myself alone. Whilst communicating with spirits who are formulating psychic phenomena, I require privacy. I need to ascertain the exact reasons for such happenings, and cannot permit distractions from other human beings at this point. The spirits need a clear channel to attain uninterrupted communication. Some disincarnate entities have personal and private reasons for creating a supernatural fuss. This spirit was such a one.

When I entered the storage area in the basement, I could see, standing against a wall, a young woman dressed in dark blue. It was a lady or perhaps a girl, who looked to be in her early twenties or late teens. She came up to me and said, 'The swine took this child from me', and holding out her hands showed me the form of a baby. She pointed to a pipe attached to a barrel and shouted, 'That's what he did to me, the bastard!' It seemed that this spirit was intimating that in the past, she had met her death at the hands of a man on these premises. I looked across at the spirit form of this young lady, she seemed forlorn and weary, but obviously intent on telling the world that in the past she had been murdered in the basement. 'Tell them I have met Kath, tell them and they will know who Kath is, she used to work in the basement, we were friends, I used to say hello to her.'

I communicated to the spirit my wishes that she return to her place which had been appointed in the next world. With her child in her arms, the spirit slowly disappeared in front of me. I felt certain that, having passed her message about a life ended by a murderer, she would be able to rest at peace in the next world. Perhaps all she wanted was for the world to know that her life had been taken by this man.

When I returned to the main part of the hotel and told Dean Hosker and the members of the press, who asked to attend, what had happened, Dean seemed absolutely amazed. Especially when I told him that the spirit had requested that I pass the name of Kath to him.

Dean's face drained totally of colour. 'Kath used to work here', he said, 'she used to do the ironing for the laundry in the basement, she always used to tell me that she could see a ghost down there.' I explained to Dean that she had been exactly right, she had seen the spirit of this young lady who had been murdered and in a way, the spirit had looked upon Kath as her friend.

I wondered, though, how the spirit could have

communicated with Kath if she had worked at the hotel, and
asked Dean what he thought about this. 'Well, Kath died last
year, she had cancer', he said. The staff who were working at
the hotel, were absolutely astonished by the accuracy of this,
though I assured them that having passed her message, the
spirit would now rest and leave them alone.

Some weeks later, Dean Hosker contacted me to say that an
old gentleman resident of Bamber Bridge, had been to see him
concerning the report in the local papers about the haunting.
They had carried the account of my psychic investigation and
details of the apparition which had appeared to me.

This man, in his late eighties, who requested no publicity,
said that he had, in the twenties, dated the girl, who at that
time had attended the doctor's surgery. For Deans Court Hotel
used to be the home and practice of a local GP. This old
gentleman recounted to Dean Hosker the story about the girl's
death. He had attended the court case where the doctor was
tried for terminating this woman's life through an illegal
abortion. She and the child were both found dead on the
premises. He was tried for their murder, found not guilty, but
subsequently struck off the medical register for malpractice.

This was proof that the information the spirit had given me
was totally correct. She had identified people who worked in
the restaurant and hotel, and recounted details of her untimely
death at the hands of the demon doctor of Bamber Bridge.

I recently contacted the Deans Court Hotel and spoke to the
co-owner, Connie. Connie told me that since the time I
attended, there had been no further psychic disturbances and
that a feeling of peace and happiness now surrounded the entire
building. The staff seemed at ease and no further supernatural
occurrences had taken place. I must say that I am very pleased
by this, and only concerned that the spirit, who had managed
to communicate her feelings of desperation about the dark deed
committed in the distant past, had found peace at last.

Living in Bolton, I meet many people who are aware of the
fact that I am a medium. Some people that I knew for many
years had, they informed me, made a pact that should one of

them die, the survivor would experience a visitation from the partner who had passed on, and that the symbol of identification would be a bird. These two people, Mr and Mrs Fred Cooper, were friends of mine for many years through the spiritualist movement.

Some years following the making of this pact between themselves, Mrs Cooper passed on to the next life. I commiserated with her husband, Fred, and assured him that in terms of spirit, his wife lived on in the world beyond the grave. Fred told me that if it was at all possible, his wife would return with evidence of survival.

Some months later, and this incident completely out of my mind, I received a telephone call at my home. It was Fred Cooper, who informed me that, on returning home from work that day, he had opened his bedroom door to see perched on his dressing table, in a sealed room, a bird. He asked if I could rush over immediately, as the creature was, at that point in time, walking around the table giving him some very strange looks. He told me that he felt certain it was the spirit of his late wife returning to prove evidence of life after death.

Fred did not live very far away from me, so within a matter of 15 minutes I was with him in his living room. However, he told me that as he had put down the telephone, having passed that information to me, the bird disappeared into thin air. It went behind a chair, and the next minute, it had vanished.

As I sat in his living room, looking across at Mr Cooper, a man I had known for many, many years, I became aware of the spirit of his late wife who was in the immediate vicinity of her husband, alive in the material world. I could not see the lady, or her spirit, but could feel the vibration of her presence. Clearly, she had returned and, in the agreed manner, proved her identity to her grieving husband who still dearly loved the woman he had known as a wife in this material world.

I explained to Fred Cooper that this would be a visitation from beyond. He could feel certain that his wife had used the agreed means of identification to enable him to be certain that in the next world she would be waiting to greet him, in the full glory of her spirit body.

Late one evening, I received a telephone call from a man I had known for some years. He requested that I go round to his flat, as he was experiencing very strange psychic phenomena.

When I arrived, he told me that as he approached the cooker to prepare his evening meal, the thing had switched itself on and the oven door opened. His kettle had begun to boil immediately, and the lights in the hallway were flicking on and off. The doors of his house were opening and closing and he was, he said, extremely frightened.

I stood in the hallway, which seemed to me to be the centre of this strange phenomenon, and became aware of the spirit of a young man. Slowly, I could see the shape of this spirit materialising by the first bedroom door. The man would have been in his late twenties or early thirties. He was of proportionate build and approximately 6 feet tall. I could hear his voice clearly now and it said, 'Tell my friend that I am with him and watching over him. I only want to let him know that I am here'.

I returned into the main room, and explained to the gentleman what I had seen in the hallway. On receipt of this news, he became quite emotional and told me that up until two months ago, he had shared the flat with his friend, who had been killed in a car accident. The description of the spirit I gave in the hallway exactly fitted the man who had lived in the house with him.

Most people are quite frightened to think that spirits are following them around. This gentleman was no different from most, in fact he was extremely perturbed, even though he knew that the spirit was that of his late friend.

Explanations are insufficient when people are scared of psychic phenomena. They simply wish them to cease. 'If he's there in the hallway, you tell him to leave me alone. I'm not used to this kind of phenomenon, and it is keeping me awake at nights', the man told me.

I returned to the site of the apparition and sure enough, waiting for me, was the spirit of the man who had lived in that flat. I knelt in prayer with him, and suggested that it was time to go to his appointed place in the world beyond. The spirit, whilst looking rather sad and wishing to maintain his presence in this material world, did agree that it was time for him to go forward and accept his new life in the world beyond.

'At first, I didn't believe I was dead, I thought that I had suddenly woken up in a strange place and was rather bemused', the spirit told me.

Obviously, this young man had returned to the place he had known best in this life, and realising now that he was in the world of spirit, had wished only to communicate that fact to his dear friend with whom he had shared that house. I was able to advise him that the best way forward to make spiritual progression was for him to follow the guide who would be sent to take him on the greatest journey of his entire existence, into the next life.

The gentleman who owned the flat received this news with great joy. I assured him that the psychic phenomena would cease forthwith, and that his house was entirely clear of this unwanted spirit, albeit that he was only there to offer him, love, comfort and affection. I believe he was sincerely delighted to hear that, and over a cup of tea, he thanked me most gratefully for helping him with what he considered to be a very bad problem of a haunted house.

It was to me the simple fact of a loved one being in the immediate presence of those he cared for and, having received the advice he required, was now able to proceed. This was a typical case of a haunted house. It happens all the time.

Another very typical example was that of a lady who lived in Blackburn. She phoned me one morning to say that during the previous night, she had been continually woken by the opening and closing of her wardrobe door. She felt that this was a supernatural phenomenon, and requested that I attend to investigate.

When I arrived at this lady's home, she told me that not only had the door of the wardrobe been opening and closing, but clothes had been removed from the wardrobe and placed on the bed. This was totally and utterly inexplicable, as she lived in the house entirely alone.

She showed me into the room where this phenomenon had been taking place. I requested that I be left alone to attune myself to the vibrations. As I heard her proceeding down the landing towards the stairs, the voice of a lady spoke to me from the side of the wardrobe.

'I used to live here', the voice said. It sounded to me as if a lady, perhaps in her sixties or seventies, was speaking. 'I was a school teacher and this was my home. That lady you have just seen is my daughter, and I want her to know that I am alive and well. Tell her I am not dead', the spirit said.

I listened to what this old woman was saying from the world of spirit. It was simply the fact that she, concerned for her daughter's wellbeing, had maintained her presence in the house that was her home in the material world.

'Tell her my name is Elizabeth and I only want to make sure she's okay', the spirit of the old lady said. I advised her that opening and closing wardrobe doors in the middle of night and removing clothes from it and placing them on the bed was hardly the way to ensure that her daughter led a happy and fulfilled life. The spirit seemed to accept this as being the truth. 'Well, I only want her to know that I am all right', she said. I explained that the lady in question was aware that she had loved her dearly in this life, and expected that in the next world, they would meet again. 'We certainly will, tell her that I will be waiting for her', the spirit of Elizabeth said.

When I recounted what I had experienced in the room upstairs to the lady of the house, she was extremely pleased and delighted that the phenomenon had been properly explained. 'I thought it was my mother. Her name was Elizabeth, and she did teach at the local school. She used to live in that room, and we were very happy together in this house. It's obvious that if she could, she would return and let me know that she loved me, because we did indeed have a very friendly and warm relationship as mother and daughter', she said.

It was simply the case that, once again, a spirit had returned to offer hope to those they had left behind in this world. The spirits, after having their position properly explained to them by me, are able to proceed to their ultimate destination in the world beyond. This is the duty of mediums, for not only do they communicate messages of hope and love from the spirit world, they are also able to advise and direct lost spirits, who are fastened by their love for others into an existence around the material world they occupied in their human forms.

This was also the truth in a case of haunting I investigated for the BBC in Bradford, Yorkshire. The date was, appropriately enough, 31 October, Hallowe'en, and the house in question was experiencing inexplicable phenomena. The presenter of the programme, which was to be broadcast live, attempted to feed me a right load of guff about headless ghosts and horrible apparitions. I never take any notice of such stories, especially when the media tell them.

Arriving at the house, I was immediately impressed by its Gothic, rather pretentious, 'Hammer House of Horror' architectural style. It looked haunted. A dark dome dominated the red brick building, which stood stark against a grey autumnal sky. 'Certainly looks the part', John said, as we entered the gloomy rooms of the ground floor. I knew at once that a presence walked the house, the question was, did it have a head?

Following an interview sequence with the owner of this strange building, I was invited to carry out a psychic search. John and I wandered round the place, which was a bit like the house that Jack built, all stairs and little rooms. If you had to describe a haunted house, this would be it. Then I felt drawn to the lower floors, as if someone was calling for me. I asked to be left alone, the spirit had arrived.

Some ten minutes or so later, I was put live on air to tell the listeners what I had discovered. The owner, standing next to me, nearly fell over when I described the presence in that unusual house. 'The spirit I spoke to told me he was your partner, he walked with a very bad limp, like this', and I demonstrated the way I had seen the spirit walk. 'He said he only had one leg', I told the owner, who by this time was staring at me in wonderment.

'You've just described the man who bought this house with me, we were going to set up a Psychic Research Centre together, then last year he died.' The explanation was perfect. 'Well, I think he wants you to continue and he's here to give you all the help he can.' The BBC couldn't fault that. Absolute verifiable proof of survival had been given, live on air. It certainly surprised the owner, but for me, it was just further confirmation that hauntings all have an explanation, and generally speaking, that explanation lies very close to the people occupying the premises.

We must all accept that life continues despite death, and if in the next world we wish to return with a message, then given the will, a way can be found. We call it, quite wrongly, a haunting. That is the simple truth of 'haunted houses'.

13

My Spiritualist Philosophy

Since the beginning of time, communication with disincarnated entities has been recorded by human beings. Indeed, the Old Testament is full of accounts in which the prophets received and communicated messages, directions and visions from the world beyond. Communication with this unseen world is not confined to the western hemisphere, it is a known phenomenon practised and recognised by races throughout the entire world.

In some lands, the interchange is both established and recorded, going back many, many thousands of years. In the Jewish religion, the Hebrew Scriptures hold much recorded data of communications received and accepted as fact by those practising that religion in the world long before Christ.

Such communication with spirit people, or 'mediumship', has no specific relation to any orthodox religious belief, understanding or teaching. It is confined by no boundaries, be they spiritual or physical (like land masses, for example). The belief in a world beyond extends throughout the globe, and has done so since time immemorial. In fact, the basis of all religions is a belief in life after death.

Through the development and advancement of society, it has become less fashionable to adhere to one specific form of religion or another, and atheists abound. However, adherents of certain beliefs consider that their particular brand of religion is the exclusive key to the next world. Some actually preach that failure to accept their doctrine will result in a life in the next world spent in purgatory or Hell. These descriptive terms are used by some to frighten and discomfort non-adherents. They warn of the dire consequences facing those who fail to accept their truth.

This is clearly false. Mediums throughout the world are aware that the spirit life exists for all of us. The only rule in the next world is truth and the love of God.

It is through the gift of mediumship that the world is permitted to glimpse the glory of the land which lies beyond the vale of death. For mediums are permitted a sight or vision of the next world, which is not readily available to the vast majority of humans. Shakespeare said in Hamlet's soliloquy that we went to 'an undiscovered country from whose bourne no traveller returns'. No doubt the Bard was expressing a philosophy in the mind of Hamlet, the Prince of Denmark. It was, however, an erroneous philosophy, for indeed travellers through the vale can, and do, return. It is the duty of mediums to enable those travellers to communicate the truth of existence beyond death.

Our departed loved ones wish us to know that life is not a one-way street, terminating in a brick wall that we refer to as death. They wish us to know, through the power of mediumship, that life continues beyond the great divide. We simply move into a different vibration and continue our existence in a life that exists beyond this material world, in which we live in our corporeal bodies.

It is the immortality of the human soul that the medium proves beyond reasonable doubt. For a good medium will offer messages and proof, certain evidence that the soul of the communicating spirit is present and passing information, through that medium, to their loved ones who remain in their human bodies. Such evidence offers to those of us remaining, hope of life everlasting. As I have previously said, this is the basis of all known religions. It should be quite clear that true mediums are able to offer factual proof. Blind faith is not sufficient; proof, actual evidence, is the essence of a true medium.

Throughout this book, I have offered illustrations of messages which I have passed to people in this world. Those messages were not mere guesses, chance ideas that popped into my mind on seeing somebody obviously distraught; those messages were given to me by spirit people wishing to prove their existence after death. It is giving this evidence, this hope and consolation, to the bereaved that is the basic duty of all mediums. We are not fortune-tellers, nor do we purport to bring false hope of joys to come. All real mediums do is to prove the existence of life beyond the grave. They bring messages from the spirit world and pass them to those who remain on earth. The facts contained in the information given should console and confirm in the bereaved a belief in life after death.

People often lead lives blighted by the fear of death. The last great adventure is certain to cause some degree of trepidation to ordinary folk who may have never undertaken any form of adventure whatsoever – let alone journeying to an unknown place entirely alone. Mediums are able to ease this worry and assure their fellow human beings that in the next world they will be greeted by those who love them.

A true medium can actually offer verifiable truth of this fact, by presenting evidence from communicating spirits to their loved ones who are seeking reassurance. The actuality of death is often followed by a short period of recognition. This varies and may be dependent on the way in which one's earthly life ended. Those who accept the truth of life after death, and are aware of their own forthcoming transition, perhaps through an acknowledged disease or illness, generally pass with ease. They understand that death is a part of their natural progression to a higher plane of existence. Being aware, they experience no shock when discovering that their earthly life is over. Perhaps the first experience a newly-passed spirit may have, which confirms physical death, is meeting with loved ones waiting for them in the spirit world. People they have known and loved who meet them with joy and affection, leading their friend on to a new life in the world of spirit.

Those whose death has been sudden, through accidents,

unlawful acts, or whatever reasons, may enter into the next life unaware that they are no longer physically alive. On arriving in the world beyond, such rapid entrants often deny that they are, in fact, dead. I have spoken to many spirits who seem quite angry that their loved ones are, in their opinion, ignoring them. The truth is that in this material world, human beings, as a general rule, only see material things. Spirits have no physical presence, no earth matter for human eyes to focus on, and are therefore invisible. However, not only can mediums see discarnate entities, they can converse with them.

One great problem for those who are unprepared for the next life is acceptance. Often discarnate spirits will continue to move in the familiar surroundings of their earthly homes, or places of work – wherever they have felt comfortable in their earthly lives. Time, which does not exist in the world of spirit, is no barrier. I believe this explains the haunted houses of England. The spirits, unaware that they are now in the next world, continue to perform the routines of their former lives, occasionally observed by a sensitive individual who reports this sighting as a ghost. I personally believe this to be especially true for those whose demise was premature. Mediums can offer guidance to such lost souls, who need only to accept the truth of their situation to begin their next life in the world of spirit.

I recall attending the home of an old lady who had told me she could see the ghost of her tabby cat which had been killed by a car some years previously. The creature, probably unaware that it was dead, simply continued as before. Often, the owners of pets who have died tell me they can sense their beloved animal friend in their houses. This is quite natural; these people are grieving over the loss and, sensing this, the spirit of the pet returns to offer comfort and love to those who cared for them in this world. Many, many times, I have heard spirit people tell me that they have been reunited with a former dog or cat that they loved in their life on earth. It matters not how many years of our time have passed between the two deaths, love is eternal. Those we have loved, be they people or pets, await us in the next life.

Life after death may prove to be initially disquieting for confirmed sceptics. They arrive, as do all spirits, into the next world and are greeted by those who are sent to guide them. The sceptic, not believing in life beyond physical death, is then faced with a real dilemma. How can they account for what has happened? They may attempt to argue through their current situation, but, assuming their scepticism is based on reason and not blind prejudice, must eventually arrive at the conclusion that they are no longer physically alive. A shock indeed, yet in my experience being physically dead does not in itself convince sceptics. I have spoken to many spirit people who are convinced that their death was a trick, and that soon they will solve the problem. I suspect that the first few weeks in the next life must be very puzzling indeed for a spirit who firmly believes that someone or something is playing a joke on them.

I recall giving a reading to a relatively young woman in Manchester who told me her husband, who had been killed in a car crash, had been a confirmed sceptic. She needn't have said anything, I could hear her husband loudly complaining that suddenly his wife had stopped speaking to him.

'Tell her, I've had enough of all this', he shouted, 'she's been ignoring me for weeks.' No wonder really, she could neither see nor hear him. I could clearly hear his complaints, and advised him that as he was now dead, he should accept the guidance his spirit friends were offering, and go on to his next life. 'I don't believe in that load of rubbish', he said. No doubt, in time, he would. When I explained this to his widow, she smiled, 'That's my husband all right, never did admit when he was wrong'.

'What happens when we pass over to the other side?' people often ask me. It is a matter which causes much concern and can disrupt the peace of an otherwise restful passing. Earlier in this book, I described how an old lady I knew spoke to the spirits of her relations, who had arrived to greet her into the next life. This, I believe, is very often the case, but it is by no means a hard and fast rule. In that particular instance, the lady simply stepped from this physical life into the other world which, for her, was populated by relatives and friends, spirits she knew. It is a fact of death that like attracts like.

Spirits have often told me that they first realised they had physically died when they met individuals who they knew had passed years previously. At the vast majority of readings I give, spirit communicators tell me they are in a world with their parents or husbands, people they have known and loved. We all have spirit guides and, generally speaking, these will be awaiting our arrival in the next world. Those guides are often members of our family who have passed before.

Communicators sometimes explain that their lives in the next world are linked to their lives in this world. I believe this to be the truth for, as I have already stated, we are the masters of our own fate, building paradises or digging purgatorial holes according to our earthly deeds. Truth and love of God rule in the world beyond, and it is only by accepting this that spiritual progress can be attained.

'Is Hell a place?' I am frequently asked. Certainly, as a medium I have never seen it. Spirits tell me that they are now living in a dark place, this they believe to be a form of Hell. I always recall my mentor, Edith Johnson Guy, telling me about judgement in the next life. 'You must face the truth, lies do not exist in the next world. As you really are, so you will be seen', she told me. Experience in communicating with thousands of spirits over the years has confirmed this to be the case. For some wicked people, whose lives have been an insult to humanity, the thought must be very frightening indeed. To be confronted with a lifetime wasted on materialism and greed, mixed in with abuse and self-gratification, must give those people nightmares. Yet face the final truth they will, resplendent in all their spiritual glory, or otherwise, as the case may be.

I have often heard a spirit say that in life they were evil people. Death alone cannot alter that, the spirit must desire to improve. Without the will to accept God's love and authority, there is then only darkness. That I believe is Hell. Yet, for each individual, I believe that Hell is different. Darkness will predominate, but their counterparts are all of the same ilk.

Thus like will attract like, until the final acceptance of God's love permits those lost souls to return to the glory of eternal light, no matter how many centuries of earth time this may take.

Hell, whilst not being a single specific place, is a gloomy reality created to improve, not punish. It must be clearly understood by all who walk this earth that, if we build for ourselves lives that hurt others, then, in the world to come, we will be confronted by our sins.

Imagine being shown the fruits of your life, and that fruit is withered and shrivelled, having been watered by the tears of those you have injured. If you live a vile and worthless life, you will see such a sight and, I believe, it will drive you to hide in the dark, so that none can see your shame. That is Hell, you can only create it for yourself. God wants you to live in the light of his love, to accept it, to repent your sins, and heaven shall be yours. It may be a long journey, but who would select an existence of oblivion, in dark dungeons dug by a life spent in wickedness and degradation.

I have heard the spirits tell me of their dark lives and I believe we should all pray for these poor foolish souls.

I accept personal responsibility for my actions here on earth. Spiritualism teaches that for each action there is a reaction. If I do someone harm, then in the next life, I must redress this wrong. Most people, I find, live lives that are relatively free from soul-damning sin. For these ordinary folk, Hell and the regions of darkness hold no threat whatsoever. So, what, I am always being asked, awaits for Mr and Mrs Average? What can an ordinary man or woman reasonably expect to find in the world of spirit? This is my understanding of the place we, in this life, call Heaven.

When the spirit or soul leaves the physical self, it retains an outward form similar to that of the body. This enables identification and permits the spirit guides to recognise their charge. Physical disabilities do, however, disappear. If someone is, for example, lame or blind, then these and any other infirmities will vanish, and will only return for identification during communication. (In an earlier chapter I explained that

I had seen a spirit with one leg. The spirits always appear to us in recognisable forms, so if people knew you as a man with glasses and a limp, then to identify yourself to friends, relatives, etc, you would return in that identifiable form. But in pure spirit body, there are no ·infirmities whatsoever.) Your spirit guide will then lead you to a land of great beauty without pain. You will not, of course, feel dead, you will feel as if you are bursting with life. For in truth we do not die, there is no death, we are simply alive in the world of spirit.

This world has many levels. As Jesus said, 'In my father's house, there are many mansions', so the exact nature of your personal mansion has been fashioned by your earthly existence, for here, only your personal worth counts.

Material fortunes are left behind on earth and your individuality shines forth, for all to see. If this is less than heavenly, then so it will be – you designed it.

Many spirits have told me that their lives were shown to them, and some were less than pleased by the experience. Others have said to me that in the next life they live in peace and harmony, surrounded by others who share their ideals. Poets speak with poets, musicians play with heavenly orchestras. I believe that your heaven will be exactly what you want it to be, peopled by those that you love.

I have yet to hear a spirit say that it would like to return to this life in a physical body. When you consider the sorrow and heartache of the material world, as opposed to the serenity of the spirit world, then the option of an instant return would seem to be less than attractive. The pain of being parted from those we love on earth is eased by the certain knowledge that in the fullness of time, we will all be together again. This fact enables new spirits to accept and proceed with life in the next world.

I recall giving a reading to one very distraught young lady, who was deeply distressed at having lost her husband. Only in his early thirties, he had suffered a massive heart attack and died. As I passed on his messages of love and affection from the spirit world, I distinctly heard him whisper to me, 'I'll be back to see you later'. But what he might want me for I could not, at that moment in time, guess.

Later that same day, I was relaxing in an easy chair, my mother out for the afternoon doing the shopping. I suppose I dozed a little, then at once I became aware of a man standing beside me. 'I told you I'd be back', he said. The spirit looked down at my seated form, and motioned for me to remain in the chair. 'I've come to show you my life in this world of spirit. Judy has been worried about me, tell her all about this and tell her that I'm okay', he said, then before my eyes there came a vision of another land.

I seemed to be standing in a long green valley, yet the hue of the grass was unlike any earthly shade. Before me were mountains, their tops dressed in snow caps, shimmering in the golden heights which engulfed the peaceful scene. Trees were there, with fruit and leaves the colour of red rubies. A crystal stream sang a song to me, it was a song of love. All about the cloud-dotted sky, birds and butterflies danced in rainbowed symmetry. 'This is my home', the spirit said, and at once appeared a gabled house of Victorian-Gothic design. The walls were hung with ivy, and before the arched doorway stood a white horse, his mane flowing in the gentle breeze. There were no other dwellings in sight, this magnificent mansion stood alone and serene, commanding a breathtaking view down the verdant valley onto the blue hills and distant mountains. The beauty so overcame me that a tear touched my cheek. Then, as if it had never happened at all, the vision vanished, I was back in Bolton on a wet Wednesday afternoon, waiting for my mother to make the tea.

I searched and searched, trying to find that lady's telephone number so that I could tell her of the vision I had of the next world, through her husband's spiritual guidance, but I never did find it. Mum must have thrown it out when she was tidying up.

Many years have passed since I saw that incredible sight which, I believe, was one of Heaven. Perhaps for each of us there will be a perfect place, but I am certain it is only ourselves who can ensure this, by living our lives decently, without hurting others, to the very best of our abilities.

Many people consider that to gain entry to Heaven they, and indeed all of us, must follow certain specific religious teachings. As I stated earlier, this is a simple fallacy invented by man, to offer hope to adherents. I can see nothing wrong in groups of people meeting once or twice, or however many times a week they like, to discuss and confirm their faith. It is, after all, not what people say that matters, it is what people do that counts. It may be that those spirits appointed to guide a devout member of a specific religious sect upon his passing were themselves members whilst on earth. This would then enable that devotee to progress without fear. In time, he would discover that doctrine is of no importance whatsoever in the great scheme of things. Mere fancies of human beings mean nothing in the world of spirit, religion and orthodox creeds, and cannot disguise a life ruined by brutish behaviour.

There are many in the world today who pay lip service to religious beliefs, yet practise profanity in the eyes of an All Seeing God. Their flimsy defence will be flipped away as the terrible truth of a life wasted is displayed for all to see. There is only one path to the Kingdom of God, a progressive path. Fine words, fancy clothes and a few hymns every Sunday morning mean zero before God. God judges deeds, not words.

One great misdeed that is undertaken by some religious movements involves the indoctrination of followers into the mistaken belief that outside their particular Church, there is no salvation. This amounts to moral blackmail. Those who practise such blatant exploitation will, I believe, be shown in the fullness of time the error of their ways. It is a pity that common sense does not prevail, and lead them away from such obvious fancies. After all, if the Muslims are right, the born-again Christians must be wrong, and if they are wrong, then where does that leave the Buddhists. It is all as one to God, whatever name we choose to call him, who requires only that we live lives of purpose and progression.

I choose to practise the ethics of Christianity: love thy

neighbour, love God, and lead pure lives free from sin. Leading a selfless life, helping others, has its own heavenly reward. Yet some use religion to reinforce social class differences. Class and wealth should, in my opinion, play no part in religious belief, but even our best-loved hymns contain reference to social status. 'The rich man in his castle, the poor man at the gate, he made them high and lowly, and ordered their estate.' Now, that is pure indoctrination, it exemplifies all that is wrong with established religion. That hymn offers only servitude and acceptance, not a world of hope, of 'all things bright and beautiful'.

As a medium, I always try to assure people that whatever their beliefs, life after death is real. To ease the suffering of the recently bereaved and strengthen their resolve to live the physical life God gave them is my duty. For we must not attempt to play God and decide our own ends. That decision belongs to a power beyond our understanding.

To commit suicide is, I personally believe, totally wrong. All the spirits I have communicated with who have passed by their own hand tell me that it was a sad mistake.

We are here for a purpose. What that is, we may not know, but God knows why we exist, and only he can decide on our appointed time. We must simply endure the hardships and problems, so often evident in this troubled life, certain in the knowledge that beyond the grave our rewards await in the world of spirit.

That is my truth, and the reason I am, and always will be, a spiritualist medium.

14
Fate Steps In

Following the response to my presentation at Leeds City Varieties Theatre, John decided that we now had the right formula for success. I had been inundated with calls from members of that audience, requesting private readings and telling me that they had enjoyed it immensely. The format had worked really well, darkness and humour interwoven to create exactly the right atmosphere. The spirits also had seemed to enjoy it, they had arrived in force, no doubt interested in what I was doing. They can see mediums very clearly, our auras shine like a bright light, guiding them to their loved ones.

The next day, my manager and I sat down together in an attempt to structure our long-term plans. We desperately needed a big tour, the theatrical presentation was in place, now all that remained was for John to make our future work. No easy task, but somehow it had to be done. To the uninitiated, it may seem quite simple and straightforward, just book the theatres, turn up and do the business. In fact, it takes very careful managing to put a tour together.

'Leave it with me, I'll sort it out', John said. I sensed he was a little worried about this. His favourite maxim, 'if I can't do it, it can't be done', was going to be tested. This was quite a challenge for one man to undertake, but in John I had absolute faith.

As I drove back home to Bolton that evening, I reflected on the occurrences of the last few months. It had been considerably less than a year since I had responded to my spirit guides' advice and called on John Sutton. Yet, in that brief time, my whole life had changed. I now felt that I was heading for the kind of success that only months before would have been unthinkable. 'You're going to be a star, my boy!', John had once told me. I laughed when I heard that, but now I believed him.

Then, as so often happens in life, fate stepped in and introduced a new player into our future. Robert C. Kelly, a theatrical agent from Glasgow, phoned to book me for a series of dates in Scotland. I referred him to my manager. Having worked for Mr Kelly in the past, I would be pleased to do so again, assuming John agreed. The telephone call that Robert C. Kelly made to my manager was to alter the course of all our lives. For Mr Kelly and Mr Sutton were two men of like minds, both accepted nothing less than success, 100% effort and determination.

Ayr, on the west coast of Scotland, is the premier seaside town north of the border. One windy Saturday in March, we set off to drive there for the evening's presentation at the Civic Theatre. It was a Robert C. Kelly Promotion, the first of our Scottish tour.

Arriving quite early in mid-afternoon, John suggested that we sit on the sea front and try a coffee, from his ubiquitous mauve flask. The wind intervened, and soon I was chasing the plastic cup along the sand-strewn promenade. John just smiled, threw his apple core to a gull and climbed back in the car. 'Can't beat a breath of sea air', he said with a subdued laugh. It was all right for him, he hadn't chased a runaway cup half a mile, in a force ten gale!

Robert C. Kelly entered the Civic Theatre, Ayr, like the master of a three-ring circus. In no time at all, he had woken John who, having managed to doze off on the dressing-room table, was less than delighted to be disturbed some hours before the start.

'Sound check! let's take it from the top!'. Mr Kelly took charge of the sound system, the lights, the stage set, the curtains, in fact, HE TOOK CHARGE! John looked on in amazement, obviously bemused by Mr Kelly's authoritarian approach. Taking me to one side, he said, 'who does he think he is, me?', recognising himself in the promoter's assertive attitude.

That evening's presentation was notable for one thing, John had prepared a pre-recorded intro-tape, which was played at the commencement of the demonstration. It was supposed to link in with our new theme of darkness and humour, and it certainly was humorous. John has quite a deep voice, and the tape sounded like a cross between Boris Karloff and Bela Lugosi gone wrong! I could hear the audience giggling as the weird music clanked with the deep bass rumble, 'there is no need to be afraid'. By this time, the curtain opened and they were openly laughing, I did feel daft.

On the way home, I asked John what he thought about Mr Robert C. Kelly. 'I begin to understand why they built that wall!', he replied, but really I knew that he was joking. He just wasn't used to being told what to do.

Glasgow's Mitchell Theatre was the next venue on our Scottish tour. The audience were lovely people who greeted me with warmth and affection. I had been warned about Glaswegians. 'They'll eat you alive, Jim', one of my friends said, recounting stories of stars who had feigned heart attacks to get off stage alive. Nothing could have been further from the truth. My messages were clear, concise and very well received, even my Lancastrian humour got a laugh. Robert C. Kelly seemed delighted with the response, and was more pleased with the second night, a total sell-out.

One message I passed at the Mitchell Theatre, was for a lady seated in the middle of the auditorium with her daughters. The communicating spirit told me, quite clearly, to warn the lady recipient that she must visit a doctor at her earliest opportunity. I passed confirming evidence verifying the spirit's identity and then, as I was requested to do, advised the lady of her urgent need.

At times like this, in a public situation, it is always difficult to speak as frankly as one might wish, tact and discretion playing a major part when messages from beyond contain warnings. In this instance, I did all that I honestly could to be truthful and impart the meaning without creating fear, or causing undue distress. The lady received the advice from her spirit communicator with great dignity. She already knew of her personal problems, and I sincerely believe the message I passed gave her hope.

That lady and I were to meet again, the next time I demonstrated my psychic gift in Glasgow. Only this time, she would be speaking from the other side.

After the two nights in Glasgow, we set off for Aberdeen's Capitol Theatre. It was quite late when we arrived in the town, which was darkening into cold night, a threat of snow in the wintry air. John pulled up alongside the first hotel we came to, time was short, so in we went. As we unpacked and prepared for the theatre, John paused to reflect on the quality of our residence. 'Jim, this is definitely a one-star hotel . . . and you're it!'. The place was freezing, my room was in the loft, overlooking a brick wall. 'It's tough at the top' I thought, wondering if the public had any remote conception of the kind of life theatricals had to lead. Many people believe it's all glamour and bright lights, but there were no bright lights in my room, in fact, the bulb had gone.

That night, at The Capitol Theatre, I received some very straightforward questions from a lady in the audience who claimed to be a medium. It seemed that she was less than impressed with my first messages. As I often say, information is often only relevant to the recipient, they alone know the truth of my evidence.

Some short time later, this 'medium's' questions were answered by the spirits. Her dead son returned to tell of a young life terminated by sniffing glue or aerosols. I described in detail the events surrounding his death, told her who was present and where it occurred, and I have no doubt there would be others in the audience for whom that information meant nothing. To the lady in question, it meant everything. She loved that boy and his wasted life had hurt her deeply.

One very pleasing aspect of our brief tour for Mr Kelly was the fact that we got paid. Robert thanked us both for our efforts and turning to John he paid me one of his backhanded compliments. 'I don't know what you've done, but he's one hundred per cent better than the last time I booked him', and with that he gave John our cheque and bid us a fond farewell.

We drove back to England, considerably more solvent than for some time. We had both enjoyed that short time spent north of the border, and I knew it would not be long before we returned and worked with Mr Kelly again.

Back in Lancashire, John Myers of Red Rose Gold Radio had contacted Mr Sutton's home asking him to phone. He wanted us back on air for an evening with his new presenter, the ex-Editor of the *News of the World*, one Barry Askew. If we had known what awaited us, the answer would have been in the negative. 'You'll like our Barry, he's a really nice man', Mr Myers had told John. We didn't. In fact, never in all my life have I been subjected to such a public ordeal. The man made James Whale seem human. I cringe at the memory of that awful interview.

Before I realised it, Mr Askew was informing his audience that 'Tonight, it's my turn to strike a happy medium. He's sitting here with a grin on his face, I'll soon wipe that off.' At that point, I very nearly got up and walked out. The only reason I didn't was that John passed me a note saying, 'sort him out'. So, without resorting to aggression, though I felt very upset at this unprovoked attack, I proceeded to defend myself. The only way I can do this on air is by proving beyond any reasonable doubt that my gift is genuine. The first call shut up the smug Mr Askew completely. This is what happened.

Barry Askew Alice, what's your question please to James Byrne.
Alice   Hello James. I just wonder if you can help me.
James   Just before we start this, have I spoken to you before?
Alice   No.
James   Right. So you are quite willing to tell the rest of

	the population of Lancashire that we have never met before?
Alice	We have never, ever met before.
James	Now, whatever I say to you, please feel free to disagree with me. I do not want you to feel that you have to agree with anything I say, unless you feel it's correct.
Alice	Right.
James	Now, if I go back about two years roughly, maybe a little bit less, I would say between 18 months and two years, there has been a terrific amount of tears that relate to a man. I do not know why that is, I am being honest about that, I do not know whether that man is living or not, but I honestly believe over the last 18 months your nightmare has been over this man. Is that correct?
Alice	Yes.
James	Do you have a son?
Alice	Yes.
James	There is a man who is with me who has died, he says his name is Billy or William. Before this man died, he had a terrible problem with his lungs or his chest and I think he had cancer. I would like to continue talking about this man, obviously his name wasn't Lily, but he did say the name, Lily. Whoever this man was and I am not pretending I know who he was, I know that he was as close to you as anybody had ever been.
Alice	Definitely.
James	It's as though he says to me, you belong to him. Now, you can take that in a lot of ways, but he definitely comes across as being that close. He told me to say to you that he can breathe better now, he's got all his weight back. Does this make sense?
Alice	Yes, definitely.
James	Does your front door have a 2 in the number?
Alice	Yes.

James	It may not be number 2 on its own, but I can definitely see a door and there is a 2 on it. Now then, is there one other number on that door.
Alice	Yes, there is.
James	This man, though I can't see him, I can hear him and he is definitely not young enough to be your son, so I would rather think he is your husband. I don't know, but I know you belong to him in some way. So, tell me what relation is he?
Alice	He's my father.
James	He's your father, so you do belong to him. He keeps talking to me about three children, now I don't know whether he means him or you. Are there three children anywhere in your immediate family?
Alice	Yes.
James	Is there a blue car parked outside your home?
Alice	Yes.
James	Is it bumped or something at the side, maybe only slightly?
Alice	No, not that I know of.
James	Is it your car?
Alice	Yes.
James	He talks about the blue car outside your home. Now I know that millions of people have got a blue car outside their home, but nevertheless, it's right, isn't it?
Alice	Yes.
James	Why can I see things to do with shops and market stalls?
Alice	I don't know.
James	Have you been buying dresses for a wedding or some special occasion that's coming up soon?
Alice	We bought some a month ago for a wedding.
James	He keeps saying something about, they look like wedding dresses to me love, but I might be wrong.
Alice	No, you're right.

James	Did you buy four dresses?
Alice	Yes, that's right.
James	That's what he said to me. Mr Askew is sick as a parrot here, but never mind.
Mr Askew	I am exceptionally impressed James, and it really is all very, very good indeed. Keep it going, it's eight and a half out of ten so far.
James	Can I just say this to you love as well. I always think again when it comes to families and relationships, it's the little things that mean a lot, isn't it?
Alice	Yes.
James	Now this guy says I have to mention parrots or a parrot? Now why would that be love, do you have a parrot?
Alice	My brother has.
James	He talks about this parrot and he said, this parrot knew the family's names. Is this right that it used to say the family's names?
Alice	Yes.
James	Do you fully understand what I have said about your dad?
Alice	Yes, I do.
James	You fully understand what I have said about the four wedding frocks and the blue car outside your door?
Alice	Yes.
James	I know what it is, he said one of your wheels, that you have just changed it, or you have had something to do with a wheel. What is it love, have you have a puncture or something recently?
Alice	No. Nothing to do with the wheels.
James	Well, what is it then?
Alice	We've just had a new exhaust on it, but nothing to do with the wheels.
James	Sweetheart, please don't worry about this, it's not serious, but please check your wheels. But you

	mustn't worry about it, it's nothing bad, if I thought it was anything bad, I would say, 'don't go in it', but I am not saying that love, all I am saying is, check your wheel. He says, it's the wheel on the driver's side at the back, so do check that love and I promise you that it's nothing bad.
Alice	Yes.
James	I know this is a common name, but who do you call Dorothy?
Alice	My sister.
James	He keeps saying, say hello to Dorothy. I obviously don't know who Dorothy is, so it's right isn't it?
Alice	Yes.
James	Obviously I don't know what's going to happen, one can only try, but I will have to leave it at that sweetheart. Thank you very much for ringing.
Mr Askew	James, as I said, eight and a half out of ten, it was remarkably impressive. Some of them, I mean, a birthday, a blue car, chest complaint.

It seemed that no matter what evidence I presented before Barry Askew, he would find fault with it. Though at the end of this ordeal, even the man himself agreed that he was impressed.

'I have never witnessed anything like this in my life', he said, 'your accuracy is between 80 and 90% beyond any chance'. I was just glad to get away. Those situations drain me terribly, I felt weak for days afterwards. Though I do believe the demonstration, conducted under very trying conditions, proved the veracity of my gift. It did more than that, it made me ask John why we agreed to be publicly ridiculed and for once, even he didn't have an explanation.

On 30 April 1992 John went with me to present at the Marine Hall, Fleetwood, a venue I had previously played in September 1991, and the first with my new manager. This time, we drew a very respectable crowd. A vast improvement on my previous date there. The opening sequence, with booming sound effects and almost total darkness, startled the audience, as many had seen my demonstrations before, but never like this. I could sense the atmosphere change as the thunder rumbled, the curtains parted and there, centre stage, stood myself, James Byrne, dressed all in black. I must admit, the public just cannot ignore that opening, it shocks them.

The messages that night were very clear and specific. The one which caused the audience to gasp most, concerned the spirit of a young boy. I could see this youth, he was perhaps nine or ten, and standing before me he led me through the auditorium to a lady, seated towards the rear right. I passed her the name of the boy. 'Tell her, I was killed by accident', the boy said, 'tell her, it hit me here', and then the spirit reached with his young spirit hand and lifted his head completely off his shoulders, placing it in my outstretched palms. I walked forward holding this. 'He's just given me his head, I've got it here in my hands, he told me this is where it hit him.' The crowd gasped in amazement as the lady recipient replied, 'Yes, he was decapitated in an accident.'

Driving home that night and listening to Red Rose Gold, I had to smile, as caller after caller were ringing Barry Askew to tell him about my demonstration. It had caused quite a sensation and, I sincerely hope, had brought belief in the truth of life after death to those who witnessed it. For that is the true reason for publicly displaying my gift. It enables the public to accept the fact of a world beyond the grave. Certainly, many people at Fleetwood that night left the theatre with hope for the future, in a new life that is yet to come.

At home, my mother continued to help me with the Saturday morning clinics. She has immense patience, my mum, except when she feels insulted. It can embarrass me at times. I generally ignore insults, or answer them by proving my gift. Mother jumps in at the deep end, both barrels blazing. One Saturday, she really made me blush.

The road I live on is often besieged on clinic days, with wheelchairs, invalid carriages, people on crutches – it looks like a scene from *Emergency Ward 10*. Then, this particular day, up our street drove this enormous great Rolls Royce, it almost blocked the narrow road, it was so large. I personally do not care who comes to see me, they all get exactly the same treatment: lawyers, schoolteachers, bus drivers, it matters not, but this man upset my mum.

The gentleman, for so he seemed, asked me to help his wife who, crippled with arthritis, could not even open her hands. 'I have to dress her now', he said, 'the doctors have told her there is nothing that can be done, you are our last hope'. I looked at this poor lady, all her fears and tears in her eyes, then, asking my spirit healers to help, I held her twisted hands. The surge of healing power I felt pass through my palms convinced me that a cure would be effected. So it was, within 15 minutes that lady regained full use of her formerly frozen fingers. She openly cried with relief. 'It's the first time they have moved in a year', she said. For her sake, I was delighted, but I do see this sort of thing all the time, to the point where I simply accept it as a fact of my psychic life.

Mother sat the couple down, along with our many other guests, and gave them a cup of tea and a biscuit. She always makes a fuss at my clinic, does mum. Then, when the lady had recovered from the surprise of regaining the use of her hands, mum got their coats ready to show them out. As the man turned to leave, he paused, reached inside his pocket and put a 50p piece on the hall table. 'Thanks', he said, and walked off towards his Rolls Royce. Mum was after him like a shot. I shuddered with discomfort, but couldn't stop her. She ran down our path like a teenager, grabbed this chap by the scruff of his neck and stuck the 50p coin in his hand.

'I think you need that more than we do, love', she said, and stamped back into the house. I was bright red with embarrassment. 'You don't let people insult you Jim', she said. She loves me, does my mum.

15

The Door Opens

The response to my first tour of Scotland for the Robert C. Kelly Agency had been exceptionally good. Mr Kelly was in fact so pleased with the results that he contacted John Sutton and suggested that in the near future, we should repeat the exercise and return north of the border for another series of presentations with himself as the promoter.

John had been applying himself to sorting out a tour of the United Kingdom for the autumn period. This, as I have previously stated, is no easy affair. Discussing our problem one afternoon in his bungalow at Leyland, he and I determined that the only way forward would be to accept the fact that alone we were unable to make the progress which we desired. So, with some reluctance, John contacted certain senior theatrical offices forwarding details of my career to date, with an outline of the potential envisaged. I understood John when he told me that the only way into the prestige venues on a structured basis was through the funding/contacts of a well-established agent. It was along these lines that we decided to proceed. What we were offering was a complete presentation, packaged, proved and ready to go. We needed the venues, we needed a tour.

Shortly after this discussion, John made arrangements to meet with some of the country's leading promoters. Then, one warm Saturday afternoon, off we set in his car and drove a great distance overland to meet just such a gentleman in his offices. No names, no pack drill, but like so many promoters, he sold us a line. When we left that office, I felt like ordering my Rolls Royce, but inside a cautionary voice said it would never happen with this man. His team had the power and, according to him, the world was definitely going to be mine. A firmer plan for progression would be forthcoming within days, and this would lead to success beyond our wildest dreams. In fact, nothing happened whatsoever. We couldn't even get a telephone call through to the gentleman we had travelled hundreds of miles to see. Why this happens is absolutely beyond me. I knew deep down, as did my manager, that this was a viable and exciting proposition which we were putting forward. Why we received such treatment, I will never know. It did concern me, but then many people turned away Epstein and The Beatles.

Following our total lack of success with senior agents established in the theatrical field, John decided on suggesting to Mr Robert C. Kelly that he consider organising a major United Kingdom tour. We had already tenuously agreed to return north of the border to tour Scotland once again for this agency. Both of us had been impressed with Robert C. Kelly's professional attitude and were pleased with the man's ability to meet his financial commitment towards us. It's always nice to be paid for one's work.

We therefore collectively agreed to approach Robert C. Kelly with the proposition that he act as our promoter. Theatrical agents and personal managers are often two separate entities which take a part in any professional presenter's life. John, whilst acting as my personal manager, organising and negotiating on my behalf, did not necessarily have to book and sign major venues for tours. After all, one man can only do so much. So, John arranged to meet with Mr Kelly and discuss the potential of our proposed venture. We wanted to ascertain his level of interest, and the extent to which he would be prepared to commit himself. This project would require dedication.

The very next week, we drove to Harrogate where, on a cool spring afternoon, we met with the Scottish impresario. John outlined our proposition with a view to getting him on our side

as an agent. He has a way with words, does my manager. Robert
C. Kelly seemed quite interested and suggested to us that in the
near future, when we return to Scotland, we should both sit
down with him and discuss the long-term potential of what we
were suggesting. I decided then to leave the matter entirely with
my manager, for it was his decision to appoint an agent, not
mine. I believe that if John said this was the right thing to do,
then that must be the case. For my part, I felt right about the
idea. No psychic alarm bells or whispered warnings, just a
feeling that this could work.

On 13 June, 1992 we were contracted to begin a second tour
for Mr Kelly, commencing at the Mitchell Theatre in Glasgow.
It was at this theatre that I had previously performed in the
month of March, and one venue to which I was looking forward
to returning.

John drove the car up to the Highlands, following the
directions given by Robert C. Kelly. Scotland is a very big
place, and Mr Kelly's inept directions enabled us to experience
a number of the more interesting sights.

Glasgow, with its tenements and teeming streets proved,
however, to be one sight that we managed to get lost in. We had
to seek advice. As John pulled into the side of the windswept
street, strewn with downtown detritus, I lowered the window
and requested directions from a passing local gentleman. None
the wiser and a great deal more puzzled, we proceeded in the
general direction of Loch Lomond. Turning right before we hit
this monstrous lake, we discovered the salubrious area of West
Glasgow, which housed Mr Kelly. His home was surrounded
by cameras and linked to an intercom system. Pushing the
button, we announced our arrival.

'What took you so long,' asked the voice of Robert C. Kelly,
'you didn't get lost, did you?' In that lilting Scottish tone, I
detected a repressed laugh, clearly he was enjoying his joke.

Robert had invited us to reside in his palatial pied–à–terre for
the duration of this tour. It was certainly an improvement on
the one-star hotel in which we had frozen on our last visit. The
only problem being that Mr Kelly's residence was up a flight

of stairs, the like of which I haven't seen since I visited the Eiffel Tower.

From the top of Robert C. Kelly's residence you could, on a clear day, see the northern lights of Aberdeen over on the right, whilst to the left the polar ice caps glistened. The whole place was like a mountain fortress. It was a long way off the ground. Very difficult for my manager, with his wooden leg, to ascend the scaffold leading to the appointed place of rest. By the time he got there, some hours later, he certainly needed it!

That night at Glasgow's Mitchell Theatre, an extremely strange occurrence took place. One of the very first messages I gave was to a gentleman in the audience. A spirit came to me and said, 'The man I want to speak to has worked at Peterhead Prison'. No sooner did I say this than I sensed a degree of agitation from a large gentleman seated in the centre stalls. With him were two young women who I seemed to have seen before.

The communicating spirit passed on messages of love and affection to the man, who was her husband, and to the two ladies, who were her daughters. As I gave them verifiable proof of the spirit's identity, the gentleman interrupted me. 'You're speaking about my wife', he said, 'when you were here in March, she was in the audience, and you gave her a message to say that she was in need of medical attention. She did accept your advice, but the doctors could do nothing to save her. She died two weeks ago.' I could see the man was overcome with emotion. The audience gasped in amazement, and even I was rather taken aback, for that lady I recall had received a warning from the spirit world concerning the state of her health. There was nothing more I could do at the time, other than to suggest she seek medical help. In the end, the inevitable took place, but I know that her spirit guides would have been waiting for her, they knew she was coming and had helped her, by passing the message I gave those few short weeks before.

As I was recovering from the import of what this gentleman had told me, I turned to seek the reaction of my manager who was in the wings. What I saw nearly caused me to drop the microphone. John was standing facing the wall with his trousers round his ankles and Robert C. Kelly was on his hands and knees, looking up at him. The audience must have wondered what was wrong with me, as I stared open-mouthed at the spectacle. This silent adult pantomime continued as those two were joined by the stage manager, a giant Scotsman who entered stage right carrying a screwdriver. Then it dawned on me, John's false leg, which had been loose all night, had finally broken and our agent, unable to fix it, had asked the technical crew to screw it back together again.

At times like those, it takes some doing to maintain one's self control and continue communicating with the spirits. It's a good job the audience didn't see it, who knows what they might have thought!

At the end of the show, the gentleman and his daughters approached me backstage to thank me for passing them what they considered to be accurate proof of the existence in the world beyond of the wife and mother that they loved. The man told me that my message to her on our previous visit had given his wife both hope and consolation. It is such acknowledgement that makes my life as a medium worthwhile, and is the reason why I will continue.

Robert C. Kelly and John Sutton were both exceptionally pleased with the way my presentation was received. For my own part, I was delighted that the recipients were able to accept those messages as being verifiable evidence of life after death, that is my only duty.

Back at the house on the hill, our impresario entertained us bachelor style. John and he attacked an innocent bottle of whisky, whilst I and our roadie, Norm, drank tea with milk. Robert C. Kelly proved a most wonderful host, but his sky palace was empty of comestibles.

'Food, I send out for it', he announced when I explained that we hadn't eaten for ages. I soon learned what he meant. Throwing me a battered, well-thumbed copy of *Yellow Pages*, Robert told me to find the takeaways and order whatever we wanted. 'I get the local taxi firm to collect my food', he said, lounging back with a single malt quad, and lemonade. 'Waste of good whisky doing that to it', advised John, who by this time had already tortured us with off-tune excerpts from Gilbert and Sullivan operas. The joys of life on the road.

By the time Sutton and Kelly finished, the place stank like an Indian curry house distillery. There were empty tins of beer, whisky bottles, glasses, jackets, shoes, a false leg, and my back was killing me.

At 6.30am John surfaced. 'Have you seen my leg?' he shouted, hopping round the room in search of his missing prosthesis. It's a good job I'm a man of peace.

The final venue of my short Scottish tour for Robert C. Kelly was at the Village Theatre, East Kilbride. This was a total sell-out, and a financial success for our Scottish impresario.

The message which remains firmly in my mind from that very successful evening concerned a young lady who had recently passed into the world of spirit. Her mother, seated in the audience, accepted the initial identifying evidence which I passed. The spirit communicating with me explained in great graphic detail the exact nature of her demise, the better to enable her relatives present to accept that in the world of spirit, she was a contented soul. The audience were extremely sympathetic to the parent, whose recent bereavement had caused her a great deal of personal anguish and pain. I recall quite distinctly explaining the nature and reason for the spirit's earthly death.

It seemed that the girl, in her mid-twenties, had suddenly experienced the sensation of internal bleeding. I could see before my eyes a vision of her last moments, she clutched desperately at her stomach and her final words were, 'Help me, mother, I am dying'. The lady in the audience accepted this, and said to me, 'That is exactly what she did say immediately before she died'. It astounded the audience and proved beyond any shadow of a doubt, that the communicating spirit was in fact that of the lady's daughter. The remainder of the message contained hope for the future and consolation in the fact that, in the world of spirit, this girl would be awaiting those that she had loved dearly in the life, albeit a short life, that she had spent on this earth.

The people of East Kilbride were extremely enthusiastic about my presentation that evening. Even the manageress, who had been initially very sceptical, agreed that this was a success. Mr Kelly was able to tell me at the interval that we would be returning at our earliest opportunity. He advised me to inform the capacity audience that we would be back in the month of July. I did this and received a welcome round of applause. Very nice people at East Kilbride, most kind.

On returning to Bolton, I was contacted by a lady called Denise, who requested that I call to see her. 'I've lost my son', she said, and told me a very sad story about a young man called Charles who had gone missing on a campsite in Canada. She told me the extent to which she had gone in an attempt to locate her only son. This she had, to date, failed to do. Having read about me in the newspapers and seeing me on television, she believed that I was potentially able to assist her in the search.

Having listened to the very strange and convoluted tale of this lady's mission, I decided that, no matter what, it was my duty to attempt to assist. So, at my earliest opportunity, I arranged to travel to her home in Yorkshire, meet Denise and give her a psychic reading, in the hope that evidence would be presented to me from the world of spirit. This is what took place.

Arriving at an exceptionally beautiful home, I was greeted by a lady who had obviously suffered immensely. Her eyes were mere shadows and the evidence of tears, shed over the years, was there for all to see. Seated in her comfortable lounge, I began to experience the presence of a spirit person, who gave me information concerning the whereabouts of her son Charles.

The spirit told me that this young man had been on a campsite in Kelownna, Canada. The man who had the answers to this problem was described to me by the spirit as being a large male with red hair, who worked in an office which was situated upstairs at the campsite. The spirit also told me that this man drove a red truck. The lady agreed with me that such a person did exist. The spirit told me of letters which had been received by Denise and gave me the surname Anthony. That is not a common surname and when I mentioned it, she seemed quite shocked. She then produced a letter post-marked Canada, which said her son's body was at the bottom of a lake, it was signed by John Anthony. 'We searched the lake, I hired a submarine, but there was no sign of my son. They did find a body, but it was that of an old vagrant.'

'Who is giving you this information from the spirit world?' she said, and when I advised her that it was the spirit of her late father, she became extremely agitated and indicated that she wanted nothing whatsoever to do with the man. There are very personal reasons why I cannot explain this further, other than to say that, in life, this man had treated Denise in a way that was unacceptable and not for public discussion.

The lady then asked me if I would watch a video, which had been taken in Canada and shown on national television there. I agreed to do this, in the hope that evidence would present itself. As I watched, I saw on the screen a man with red hair and as soon as I saw him, I heard the spirit say to me, 'That is the man who has the answers to this boy's whereabouts'. When I told her, she explained that this was the person who ran the campsite. 'Get this man before the police, he knows exactly what has happened to your son. The spirits have told me that he was present during this boy's disappearance.' I gave her this information, along with many other pieces of evidence which were passed to me by the spirits.

I tried sometime later to contact Denise and ask her opinion of the evidence I had given her. But, from that day on, I have never been able to speak to her. I believe that she has left the country, potentially to seek out the gentleman I indicated as having the answers necessary to solve the mystery of her missing son.

I think Denise must have contacted the press, for within a matter of days, the news was headlines. PSYCHIC'S CLUE TO MISSING BOY said the papers. That essentially was not the case, I had simply passed on the information which I had received from the spirit world. If this was eventually responsible for solving the case, then in some way, I have managed to play my part. I can only hope that this lady finds in that solution the peace for which she is so obviously searching.

So many people need help. The day after that story hit the papers, I was snowed under with calls asking for assistance in finding missing persons. My mother handed me a note when I went home for the evening meal. It said 'please phone urgently, woman desperate', and gave a local telephone number.

'The woman sounded near to hysteria, you'd better ring her Jim, I said you would.' Mother is always anxious to assist. So, I phoned and was surprised to hear an old lady explain in minute detail the characteristics of Marmalade, her tomcat, which had disappeared some weeks before. 'Do you think you can help me find him?' she asked. As we spoke, a vision of her cat returning came before my inward eye, and the day Friday came into my mind. 'Back on Friday', I told her. Sure enough, on Friday next, she phoned my mum to tell her the good news. 'Eh Jim, how do you do it?' she said. Mum thinks I'm some sort of genius.

My manager phoned me early one Monday morning to suggest a meeting. 'I have a dream!' he said, 'We're going to open all the doors, I have developed a plan. Come and see me tonight.' Well, we certainly needed something, and for sure, it would never knock on the door one starry night, that only happens in the movies. It was up to us to make sure it happened, but I had no idea what John had in mind. No doubt it would be something dramatic.

I told my mum that Mr Sutton had a dream that we would succeed. 'Can he make me famous too?!' she joked. In the back of my mind, a voice whispered to me, 'Yes'. When I told mother that, she did laugh. 'And what will I be famous for, James', she said, 'washing your socks and making tea?' But without mum's help and understanding, I could never have continued as I have done. 'You'll see mum, I know it's going to happen, I have been told', I said. Yet I did wonder just what John had got up his sleeve. That evening I was going to find out.

Arriving at John's home, near the duck-dipped pond, at

Leyland, I sensed that something important was about to occur. He opened the door with his usual cheery grin, grabbed me by the arm and said, 'Come in Superstar and sit down. Mary, make my boy a cup of tea, we're about to change his life.' I had seen John certain in the past, but this time, he was definitely bursting with enthusiasm. 'You, my boy, are about to become the Most Famous Psychic in the World!' John said. I looked across at him and despite my great faith in this man's ability, I somehow doubted that what he had told me would eventually transpire, although I had great hopes.

'How you would like to play the London Palladium?' John said. I nearly dropped the tea that Mary had just given me. This would be a dream come true. I had always wished to play that prestigious venue, probably the most famous theatre in the entire world, and John was now suggesting that we undertake that extraordinary adventure.

'How are we going to do that?' I asked him.

'Quite simple, I have spoken to Robert C. Kelly and we are starting a major 40-date tour of the United Kingdom, commencing on the 27th September 1992 at the London Palladium. James Byrne SUPERSTAR!' John said with an air of authority in his deep bass voice.

During our extraordinary meeting, John explained to me that during the day he'd had lengthy discussions with Robert C. Kelly concerning our future business arrangements. He had agreed, on my behalf, that we work exclusively with the Robert C. Kelly Agency, on the understanding that Robert write in the London Palladium as the start of our major tour. This Mr Kelly had agreed to do, and during that day had confirmed the booking with my manager, who was now in a position to advise me that my dream, which I had held for 20 years, was most certainly about to be realised.

I could see that John was as excited about this proposition as I was. 'How on earth have you persuaded Mr Kelly to do this?' I asked him.

'Simple', he said, with one of those manic glints in his eyes, 'I just told him, no Palladium, no deal', he replied.

'What did he say to that?' I asked.

'That, my dear boy, is not for sensitive ears such as yours', John said with a deep guttural laugh.

Whatever way he had done it, it seemed that John had indeed managed to open the doors, and for that, I will forever be grateful, not only to the man himself, but also to my spirit guides for indicating the pathway that was there. For I believe that without my guides' intervention, the future would have been entirely different. Before I went to see John, I was fighting a losing battle. Now, after less than a year, I was on my way to success. All this was obviously meant to happen.

When I got home that night and told my mother, she was absolutely delighted. 'Oh Jim, you are going to be a star!' she said, giving me a hug and placing a hot cup of tea in my hand. For once, I actually believed that this might now be the case.

Later that night, as I sat contemplating life, and the way fate and fortune had worked out for me, I recalled my early years. Edith Johnson Guy had predicted that my future would be as a medium and once, perhaps ten years ago, this had been verified by Gordon Higginson.

Gordon, the President of the Spiritualist National Union, came to see me at the end of one of my church demonstrations and said, 'James, your mediumship is right now, continue and you will go a long way'. Experience tells me that when Gordon Higginson speaks, he speaks the truth. He is the one medium I admire, above all others.

I could hear my mum clattering about, rattling the pots and pans as she prepared our supper. In the near distance, a car accelerated into the purple summer night and I remembered things past. For me, life was about to change, I had turned a different corner and things would never be the same again.

'Do you want some more tea Jim', mum shouted from the kitchen, 'and a piece of toast?' I bet you don't get that kind of service at the Palladium!

Of further interest . . .

Living Images
THE STORY OF A PSYCHIC ARTIST

Coral Polge

Coral Polge has a unique gift. While most clairvoyants describe communicators from the spirit world, she takes communications one step further and actually transmits onto paper an image of the spirit with whom she is psychically in touch, much to the amazement of the relatives of the departed.

In this updated edition of her autobiography, trained professional artist Coral Polge describes how she has come to terms with her psychic gifts. Harnessing her artistic prowess to her mediumship, she has become famous internationally for her singular talents, formerly Spiritualist of the Year and now constantly in demand all over the world.

A Londoner by birth, she tells the story of her life with honesty and humour, from an ordinary childhood background, through personal and professional progress, to her current status, ranked high in the psychic field. She does not shy away from telling of the many problems she has encountered along the way, and describes her simple and logical philosophy of how and why her gift operates.

'Seek the Truth,' Coral's spiritual guides told her in her early days. She sought and found — and now she reveals her findings which will strengthen the believers and confound the sceptics.

Out of My Hands
MY LIFE AND WORK AS A HEALER

Allon Bacon

Allon Bacon's story is a colourful account of a man whose life as a healer enables him to give a unique insight into the fascinating world of spiritual healing.

His early days as a medical student cut short by tuberculosis at the beginning of the Second World War, Allon Bacon was saved by his discovery of powers of self-healing. During the course of his later career, writing and composing for the theatre in Britain and France, he developed his psychic awareness. Coming to accept his own healing powers and their significance, he later brought them to benefit an increasing number of people in many walks of life and more than one country. A wide variety of public names show up in these pages as they play their brief or longer parts in this intriguing life story.

Leading the reader through the curious world of psychic experience and phenomena in a down-to-earth manner, he tells how healing works, describes several of his own healings and goes on to teach self-healing techniques and meditation.

Out of My Hands will uplift the sick, lonely and ailing, inform the successful, fit and strong, and serve as a source of inspiration and guidance for those seeking self-awareness and the power to heal.

Edgar Cayce
A SEER OUT OF SEASON

Harmon Bro

Gifted since childhood with the ability to enter into a trance-like state of consciousness, Edgar Cayce could diagnose illnesses he had never studied, cure ailing people he had never met and prescribe successful treatment without any formal medical training. His powers of prophecy and his ground-breaking psychic perceptions stunned a sceptical nation four decades before the New Age Movement.

This fascinating biographical memoir, written by a leading scholar and longtime disciple of Edgar Cayce, sheds new light on the most gifted psychic of our time. Drawing on hundreds of interviews with relatives, associates, disciples, even sceptics, this definitive work is the first to view the whole of Cayce's life, taking into account his journals, dreams and lectures, case studies of those whose lives were miraculously altered by his ministrations, his riveting descriptions of what he called his reincarnated lives, and the four areas of his contribution to contemporary life and thought: ESP, holistic health, reincarnation, and disciplined spiritual growth.

In this landmark book, Edgar Cayce, 'the Father of the New Age,' emerges not merely as a medium or a mystic, but as a modern-day seer, albeit a lonely one, isolated by his burdensome gifts and by the awe he inspired in others. Yet in a world that now possesses the terrifying ability to destroy itself, Cayce's timeless ideals of faith, healing and peace may have finally found their season.

LIVING IMAGES Coral Polge	1 85538 084 6	£4.99 ☐
OUT OF MY HANDS Allon Bacon	0 85030 831 3	£6.99 ☐
EDGAR CAYCE Harmon Bro	0 85030 937 9	£9.99 ☐
VISIONS OF ANOTHER WORLD		
Stephen O'Brien	0 85030 836 4	£4.99 ☐
VOICES FROM HEAVEN Stephen O'Brien	1 85538 078 1	£4.99 ☐
THE TRUTH VIBRATIONS David Icke	1 85538 136 2	£4.99 ☐
LOVE CHANGES EVERYTHING David Icke	1 85538 247 4	£4.99 ☐
NOSTRADAMUS J.H. Brennan	1 85538 145 1	£5.99 ☐

All these books are available from your local bookseller or can be ordered direct from the publishers.

To order direct just tick the titles you want and fill in the form below:

Name: _____

Address: _____

_____ Postcode: _____

Send to: Thorsons Mail Order, Dept 3, HarperCollins*Publishers*, Westerhill Road, Bishopbriggs, Glasgow G64 2QT.
Please enclose a cheque or postal order or your authority to debit your Visa/Access account —

Credit card no: _____

Expiry date: _____

Signature: _____

— up to the value of the cover price plus:

UK & BFPO: Add £1.00 for the first book and 25p for each additional book ordered.

Overseas orders including Eire: Please add £2.95 service charge. Books will be sent by surface mail but quotes for airmail despatches will be given on request.

24 HOUR TELEPHONE ORDERING SERVICE FOR ACCESS/VISA CARDHOLDERS — TEL: **041 772 2281.**